JOHNNY
HERBE...

GW00375157

Other books by the same author:

AYRTON SENNA
His full car racing record

NIGEL MANSELL
The Lion at Bay

MICHAEL SCHUMACHER
Defending the Crown

GERHARD BERGER
The Human Face of Formula 1

AYRTON SENNA
The Legend Grows

JAMES HUNT
Portrait of a Champion

GRAND PRIX SHOWDOWN!
The full drama of the races which decided
the World Championship 1950–92

TWO WHEEL SHOWDOWN!
The full drama of the races which decided
the World 500cc Motor Cycle Championship
from 1949

TORVILL AND DEAN
The full story

JEAN ALESI
Beating the Odds

JACQUES VILLENEUVE
In His Own Right

As part of our ongoing market research, we are always pleased to receive comments about our books, suggestions for new titles, or requests for catalogues. Please write to: The Editorial Director, Patrick Stephens Limited, Sparkford, Nr Yeovil, Somerset BA22 7JJ.

JOHNNY
HERBERT

THE STEEL BEHIND THE SMILE

Christopher Hilton

Patrick Stephens Limited

First published in 1996

British Library Cataloguing-in-Publication Data:
A catalogue record for this book is
available from the British Library

ISBN: 1 85260 562 6

Library of Congress catalog card no. 96 75831

Patrick Stephens Limited is an imprint of Haynes Publishing,
Sparkford, Nr Yeovil, Somerset BA22 7JJ.

Designed and typeset by G&M, Raunds, Northamptonshire
Printed in Great Britain by Ebenezer Baylis & Son Ltd,
The Trinity Press, Worcester, and London

Contents

Acknowledgements   6

Straight from the grid   7

CHAPTER ONE: In the kart   11

CHAPTER TWO: Cheeky chappie   36

Colour pages   65–80

CHAPTER THREE: The battering   81

CHAPTER FOUR: The rack   116

CHAPTER FIVE: Rebirth?   146

Appendix: Johnny Herbert's career statistics   151

Acknowledgements

MANY PEOPLE HAVE helped, and I'm grateful to them all, but I must single out Bob and Jane Herbert for their candour and humour as well as their memories. Sincere thanks, also, to Bill Sisley of Siskart Limited, Buckmore Park, Kent; Eddie Jordan and Trevor Foster of Jordan Grand Prix; Mike Thompson of Sample Surveys Limited; Marcus Pye of *Autosport*; Mike Langley, Perry McCarthy, Ian Blackman, Mike Baker; Danny Miller of Brands Hatch, and Marion Day, Sue Page and Neil Harper of the Brands medical staff.

Mark Burgess of *Karting* magazine, Anita Smith of Reynard Cars and Maurice Hamilton of *The Observer* acted as valuable conduits. Simon Taylor, Chairman of Haymarket Specialist Motoring Publications Limited, kindly gave permission to quote from *Autosport*. David Hayhoe cast a knowing eye over the statistics and helped make them more complete than they would have been. I have also used his comprehensive *Grand Prix Data Book* extensively, which was of particular comfort to the author.

On a strictly personal level, thanks to Johnny Herbert himself for years of irreverent interviews, agreeable verbal sparring and — at important moments — speaking the truth, whether it was in his interests or not.

Straight from
the grid

MID-SUMMER 1996 — a difficult time, as it happened — and someone asked Johnny Herbert to describe himself in three words. 'Very laid-back,' he replied, and no doubt accompanied it with his impish, semi-naughty choirboy smile. He conjures this smile in good times and bad, but you can never be sure if he is not using it as a shield to mask what he really feels. A close friend, as we shall hear, has only known Herbert to be visibly angry a bare handful of times in more than ten years, and he expressed the anger by going very quiet and not smiling.

There is much more to Herbert than the superficiality of facial expressions, of course. That is what this book is about — the more — and why it is called what it is. You must have seen the smile yourself — when he won the Le Mans 24-hour race in 1991, when he won the British Grand Prix at Silverstone in 1995 or, two months later, added the Italian at Monza — and wondered what lay beyond it.

You may also have glimpsed him stumping along with, in his own words, his bum sticking out and wondered about that: his limp is the physical echo of 1988 and what may well have been the worst multiple motor racing crash of the decade. Up to the moment of the crash he had been a gifted driver who found winning quite natural, although he wasn't sure why he could make fast cars go so fast. Here is a fragment of my conversation with his parents:

Bob: The first time he drove a Formula 1 car — a Benetton at Brands Hatch — I think Ayrton Senna was quickest, Nigel Mansell next and Johnny third. I think he was four-tenths of a second off Senna and three-tenths off Mansell. He was quicker than experienced drivers like Derek Warwick and Thierry Boutsen.

Hilton: The power of the car wasn't too much for him.

Bob: You've got to think he was being put in a Formula 1 turbo car and the most he'd been driving was Formula 3.

Jane: The point was, it was a tight circuit, there were other Formula 1 cars on it — he hadn't been given an empty circuit and left alone to learn — so he had to be aware of these other cars as well as everything else.

Hilton: What is this ability — where does it come from?

Jane: I can't tell you what it is. I've asked him and he says he can just do it.

Bob: It was just something that happened the first time he went in a kart when we were on holiday in Cornwall, it was something he just took to.

Jane: Yes, he could do it . . .

Bob: He didn't learn to drive a car by having lessons. When we'd arrive at a circuit for the kart races I'd jump out of our car and he'd take over and drive the rest of the way into the circuit, might be a hundred yards, might be a mile.

Hilton: And he could do that, too.

Bob: Oh, yes.

Nobody does know where the ability comes from — in the early days we're talking about winning a lot in karts; winning the Formula Ford 1600 Festival from the back of the grid (which received wisdom decreed could not be done); winning the British Formula 3 Championship so easily that Eddie Jordan, running him, remains sure that Herbert slowed in the races and let the others catch him to make it more interesting (which enraged Jordan); mastering Formula 3000 instantly. Equally, nobody knows what effect the crash of 1988 had. It mangled his feet so badly that amputation was a real possibility and, although that wasn't necessary, the recovery would inevitably

A long year from the triumph of 1995 at Silverstone to (above) ninth place in 1996 (Formula One Pictures).

always be less than total; which, in turn, makes you wonder. Braking in a Formula 1 car — late-braking, invaluable for gaining time — requires of the foot both strength and sensitivity. I don't want to make too much of this because Herbert is approaching a century of Grand Prix races and finished fourth in the 1995 Championship. With the mobility/immobility of the foot we're only talking about small degrees — but success in Formula 1 is itself often about small degrees.

Certainly the momentum of the career was slower after the crash than before it; and it was then — for someone whose self-portrait is laid-back, chirpy and wreathed in that smile — a curious career: physical agony at Benetton the first time round, four years of anguish at Lotus, an almost bitter season at Benetton the second time round, a slog through 1996 with Sauber when his team-mate Heinz-Harald Frentzen, *regarded by some as faster than Michael Schumacher*, did not decisively out-drive him.

9

These days Herbert lives in Monte Carlo with wife Becky and daughters Chloe (born January 1990) and Aimelia (July 1992). No doubt his upbringing in Romford seems a long way away — although you can wonder about that, too. He has not compromised how he behaves to accommodate Formula 1 fame, or money, or Monaco. For example, during all his tribulations during 1996, rather than slink off moaning and mumbling, he was constantly prepared to face the BBC's man in the pit lane, Tony Jardine, and discuss frankly what had gone wrong. Herbert insists that he is 'very hard to embarrass' anyway, but that's not the point. He remains approachable even in adversity and is truly no slinker; but more important, he is quite prepared to say *I made a mistake* if he made the mistake. This is not, let me say, standard practice in Formula 1.

He is fatalistic. He likes the idea of fate. That is surprising for a racing driver because your perception of the species is that they need to be a) impossibly positive and b) powerfully motivated to cut their very own path through all known obstacles. The notion of fate as something you cannot control is the opposite. Again as we shall hear, gauging whether this has helped the career or hindered it is difficult, but the fatalism is an integral part of the man.

So is a hardness that is rarely paraded for the public view. A rare example was when Herbert launched several savage, detailed and heartfelt broadsides against Benetton over how he had been mistreated in 1995. Herbert was unafraid of doing this, because he felt a need to explain why team-mate Schumacher had been going so much faster in theoretically an identical car, *and* he felt a deep need to articulate what he regarded as unfair play — as if such a thing violated Herbert's basic beliefs. This hardness runs through the book virtually from the beginning and, as someone says, if a team gives him what he judges he needs he'll give 100% in return and no worries; if he thinks he is not getting what he needs you'll see the cherubic face and it will not be smiling.

Another part of the story is captured by Monaco 1996 when, absurdly, only three cars were still going forward at the end, Herbert one of them. It was a consistent, calm, calculated performance, mature and sensible, a maximising of the possible. When they got round to shaking and squirting the champagne the smile was as wide as the harbour . . .

CHAPTER ONE

In the kart

JOHNNY HERBERT'S LIFE in motor racing began exactly as so many others have begun: on holiday, by chance and at minimal cost — in that order. He was eight.

Parents Bob and Jane had taken him and his sister Sarah to Cornwall to visit Bob's sister and brother-in-law, who ran a holiday complex on what had been an RAF base. It included a typical kart track, a snake of a circuit fashioned by tyres on a long-disused runway. A fun circuit, as they say. Bob Herbert, an electrician by trade, had never seen a kart before and knew nothing about them.

Johnny made an inevitable request. 'Can I go on that, daddy?'

'Yes, OK, but watch yourself and be careful.'

Johnny sat on the kart and set off down the contorting corridor between the tyres, went round and round, returned. 'It won't go fast enough.'

Bob wasn't particularly interested in this karting, and if his sister and brother-in-law had possessed, say, a boating lake or a riding school instead, it would have been the same thing to him. You take whatever facilities are on offer, and Bob judges that it was 'fate' that it happened to be karts. Certainly there was no history of motor sport in the family.

Understandably, because anyone could hire a kart and they are potentially dangerous machines, the throttles were tied up to prevent excessive speed. Little Johnny was family, however, and they untied the throttle and he went off again a lot faster; and because little Johnny was family the question of paying for lap after lap didn't arise, so he kept on.

He hasn't stopped since. These many years later, Jane is grateful that he found an outlet for his energy and a discipline to control it. He was, she insists, hyperactive virtually from birth on 25 June 1964 at Romford.

'He was always tearing about, flying about,' she says. 'He'd sit in his pushchair in the back garden and rock it backwards and forwards until he'd got to the other end of the garden. At 18 months old he'd clamber out of his cot and Bob said *it's too far to fall* so we let the side down' — meaning the little ball of energy could descend properly rather than tumble over the top.

'He'd get on to the bedroom windowsill and children playing in the street used to knock on the door and say *Mrs Herbert, he's on the windowsill again!* He was probably being a bit of a showman. I don't know if that's exactly what you'd call it, but he was always like that. When he was about two he was in the back garden but he wanted to play outside it. I'd locked the gate, of course, to keep him in. He climbed on to the neighbour's coal bunker and got out through her garden . . .'

Bob remembers vividly that 'he was always an angelic-looking little child with long blond hair down to *here*. When he was a baby in the pram people would go *ah, ah, ah* and I think somehow he learned to play up to that — he enjoyed that. Then when he went to school he was still this little angelic child. Most people thought he was a girl, not a boy . . .'

'. . . and that was even at 11,' Jane says.

'Anyway, people always used to go *what a lovely little child, what a lovely little child*, and perhaps he did learn to play up to that.'

Jane says that at school 'the problem was — and a male teacher summed this up for me — he brings out the motherly instincts of the female teachers.' From this I deduce, especially since all are agreed that The Angel was strong-willed, that he got away with a lot. Certainly Bob and Jane wouldn't let me see his school reports,

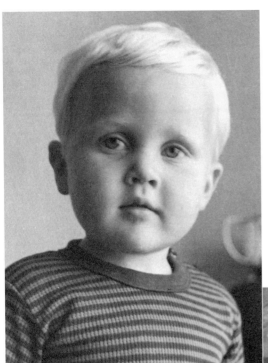

Two rare studies of Herbert as a little lad. He's motionless! (Herbert family).

although I'm shockproof, because I've a collection of authentic shockers of my own.

'In those days' — the time of the visit to Cornwall — 'he was interested in football at school, but they didn't have under-10s in an organised way,' Bob says. 'In the karting he had found himself an interest, and when we came back it was a question of buying him one. I had no idea where to look. I bought *Exchange and Mart*, and there was a kart for sale at Redhill near Gatwick Airport. It was a vicar's kart! I think he'd got it for the local boys to go round and round the vicarage. We went down there, saw this kart and I didn't know what I was looking at.'

He had so much energy and I think the karting channelled it

Johnny remembers 'my father buying me my first kart. It was quite funny really. We got it from this clergyman. We were imagining him conducting the Sunday morning service, whipping off his dog-collar and heading off to do fierce battle and bang wheels in the afternoon. We thought we had better take it off him . . .'

Bob remembers that 'there was an engine on this old kart, but there should have been two: a twin-engined kart. There was also a box of bits. I paid £35, something silly like that, because I wouldn't pay a lot of money. We then found out there was a circuit at Tilbury — in actual fact, as I discovered later, the first circuit in the country — and we'd go down on a Saturday and he'd drive round and round in circles.

'The other karts there were owned by racing types who'd brought them to practice. Ours was like an iron bedstead. It had a metal seat which was part of the kart. We never did get the second engine up and running from the box of bits for it. I remember once he was coming down the straight and one of his wheels overtook him — it had just sheared off! We got it welded and off he went again. That's how it was, and we had this kart for quite some time. And you get talking to people, don't you?'

Yes, you do. Even silent types in motor sport talk a lot because there is constantly a lot to talk about, and — like the driving round and round every Saturday — it's like an induction. Almost before you know it, you're *in*. Most never do find the way out, mainly because they're not looking for it. Quickly enough, they *need* to stay in.

For this, Jane Herbert is truly grateful. First, she believes the physical and mental discipline was an excellent way of harnessing the hyperactivity. Second, 'I don't think he would have been around with us if it hadn't been for the karting.' Meaning? 'Well, he had friends, he'd have gone off with them and we wouldn't have been so close. I'm not saying if he'd gone off he'd have been naughty because he wasn't a naughty boy — always liked his school and everything, although he was a bit of a *pickle*.' Meaning? 'Well . . .'

Bob is grateful, too. 'He was just full of energy. He had so much energy and I think the karting channelled it. I enjoyed it because I started learning to tinker with the kart. I was beginning to work with him. Before that I was working all the hours at my job and I didn't see much of him. Sarah was never interested in it, but she'd always come along and enjoy the social side, so it was all something you do for your kids. We enjoyed the social life and everything else that went with it.'

One of the more senior karters was giving up — he had a 'proper kart so we bought this proper kart. Because Johnny's feet were so small we used tobacco tins to get him to reach them.' Meaning? They put two tobacco tins under the pedals so he could rest his feet on them, and made 'little aluminium guards' around the front of the tins so his feet didn't slip off. 'We brought the seat forward as far as you could and packed it out with cushions to get him even further forward to reach the steering wheel, because they didn't make karts for youngsters, you see, and he was little anyway.

'The kart had a real racing engine and he'd go tearing round, mainly at Tilbury but also over at Rye House [used for speedway and stock cars, also]. I think it used to cost £5 a day. It was money, but that's all we ever did, you know. Because we only went on a Saturday, it represented £5 a week plus your bits [food and petrol]. Then he'd bomb round as much as possible.'

The talking at Tilbury turned to a question. *Why isn't the boy racing?* Bob Herbert understood that, at 10, Johnny wasn't old enough. You had to be 11. Bob didn't really understand licences from the RAC and so forth, and why should he have done? What he did understand was that other kids were racing and Johnny was getting 'fed up' going round and round going nowhere. Moreover, he met the parent of another karter who said *ah, Johnny not old enough? Don't worry about things like that. Just send off for the licence.* 'That is what we did.'

What Bob Herbert ought to have done was get into forgery. 'How you do that I was told afterwards, but nobody told me before. A birth certificate is like a marriage certificate. You always show a photocopy of it. So what you do is — and this is very interesting for any bugger who wants his kids to race (laughter) — photocopy the birth certificate then Tipp-Ex out the date and write the date you want, then photocopy it again. You have a proper copy of a birth certificate with a forged date which you can show to anybody, proving you are 65 or 66 or 67 or whatever.'

Because Bob Herbert did not know the Tipp-Ex treatment, he tried forging forms with the signatures of clerks of courses and dates. His fate was the fate of an honest man. One date he got it so spectacularly wrong that an official wondered how his son drove so well at the age of two weeks . . .

A word of explanation and vindication. Let me stress that forging to get your son into a kart race is not in any way the same as forging, say, bank notes; and a healthy scepticism about rules and regulations is almost a prerequisite for a life in motor sport, anyway.

Inevitably the Herberts were rumbled. This happened at a meeting at Morecambe attracting, among others, young hopefuls. Some of the more experienced runners had *gearboxes*, which not all karts have and which angelic J. Herbert had not.

'I walked into the circuit and it was literally on the edge of a cliff,' Bob says. 'It frightened the life out of me. I said *you're not racing here.*'

Bob remembers a great big dirt lane if you didn't get round the hairpin — they'd laid two old doors as banking, and if you missed the doors or the doors had been removed 'you'd go over the top of the cliff'.

Conversation:
J. Herbert: 'I want to race, I want to race.'
B. Herbert: 'You are not going to race, you are not going to race.'

Compromise:
B. Herbert: 'All right, we'll see how it goes.'

Preparing to rock'n'roll to the other end of the garden? (Herbert family).

Authentic Herbert: action (Herbert family).

Rumours passed round — 'A few people said *there are a lot of people talking about your boy*. Nobody actually came down and said he couldn't race. The fact is he did best of all the juniors. When we got home I received a letter from the RAC asking me to produce his birth certificate. This is where I couldn't produce it. If I'd done it like everybody else [the photocopy/Tipp-Ex route to time travel] I'd have simply sent a copy off, but I thought *I can't*. If you don't produce the birth certificate you can't race. They sent a letter out to all the kart circuits saying *don't accept this kid's entry until he is old enough*.'

Bob duelled with the RAC because they said it was a matter of insurance, to which he riposted, 'That is ridiculous because young kids are doing scrambling and everything at seven years old. They are breaking their shoulders, they are breaking their arms.' As an outsider, this would seem to me a very good reason for not insuring seven-year-olds, but never mind. Bob 'really fought, and then they brought the age down after a lot of my campaigning. They brought out a new class which was Junior Britain.'

Johnny was small, even for a junior. One race report said 'all you could see was a *helmet* flying round', the body under it too small to be visible.

Bob says that 'once we started racing we bought an old 10-foot caravan which we parked at the circuits, and it was good fun.'

A chap called Bill Sisley was at Morecambe. He was invited into the caravan and he and the Herberts briefly came to know each other. Sisley was worth knowing because he sold karts and parts.

'I approached Bill [for help] and Bill didn't want to know, sort of thing, I suppose because the kid was too young to put money into. Then John was banned. He got his licence when he was 11 and I phoned Bill from a call-box in Sidcup, where I happened to be, and I think he still said no. I phoned him because I couldn't afford to pay for the racing on my own.'

Bob Herbert decided it was time to meet Sisley again face to face.

'We were getting serious, yes.'

That day in 1975 Sisley was working in his shop in Swanley, Kent. A customer had come in and now stood at the other side of the counter. The customer wore his hair long, was 'a very down-to-earth

Right *Smile, please, Bob, Jane, Johnny and Sarah* (Herbert family).

18

Essex chap', and Sisley recognised him from the visit to the caravan.

Bob moved into an incantation. *My son John, he's 11, he's the greatest, he's going to be world champion.* Sisley no doubt nodded with just the right touch of gravity because he'd heard these words so often from so many parents and had devised a straightforward method of dealing with them: *Yes, yes, yes, but let's see the kid in action and then we'll see what we see.* As Sisley stood on his side of the counter he did not realise that Bob had brought John, who 'was so small I couldn't see him over the counter'. When Sisley did see him, blond hair and the rest, he thought Herbert looked 'angelic' — that word again.

'Bob had come to talk about buying a kart for Johnny, and I said, "Obviously I'd love to sell you one," but he said, "We haven't got much money", which is the normal thing. I said, 'OK, let's see him drive first.'"

Sisley arranged a test. 'The track, what we call a club kart track and measuring 600 metres, was at Tilbury, and we did most of our testing there. He was tiny and we had to move the pedals so he could reach them.

'I can tell within five minutes whether someone is going to be very good or not very good. What you can't tell is whether they'll be good enough to make a career of it — that takes three or four years. Initially they have to have natural aggression and skill, and, if anything, they drive too quickly not too slowly. In time they learn to slow down, and in doing that they become quicker [control = smoothness = speed]. At a test like this I'd never say a driver is bad — I'd be more diplomatic about it — but anyway I thought *he's good.* I could tell that. My main concern was how quick he could eventually be, and, as I say, you can't judge that immediately.'

What followed was what Sisley describes as 'a deal, because different factors always come into play which make things happen, don't they? In Johnny's case it was purely coincidental, but we were thinking about manufacturing karts rather than just be what we had been, agents for other karts.

'My brother-in-law was an engineer and he wanted to design a kart for us to sell. I had my doubts that an engineer who knew nothing about karts could provide one that worked, but he was insistent and on that premise I discussed the situation with Bob. The idea would be to let Johnny drive it. That way it wouldn't cost me any money

Action 1977, at Surbiton (Herbert family).

because my brother-in-law would have financed it and Johnny would have learned how to drive — and it wouldn't cost the Herbert's anything: Johnny was test-driving the kart, he was developing the kart and I was doing some testing with it as well. That's what did happen.

'The kart was called the *Tarantella* [after a whirling south Italian dance] and basically it didn't work. It was unique in the sense that most kart frames were ladder frames, but this had the central section of one piece. There was no width, it was very stiff in the middle and wouldn't handle consistently, but we persevered with it, Johnny and me, for maybe two years. Then my brother-in-law lost interest. I

21

approached a friend called Vic Gray, whose son competed. Vic was an engineering man near Ashford and he said, "OK, I've got a little factory that I want to use for something. Why don't we make karts? I'll design them and you sell them." That's how the *Kestrel* and *Cobra* karts were born.'

Did you pay Johnny money?

'Yes, peanut money because, the way it was, all the other money was going into his racing. You must remember that even in 1974, 1975, when you reached the higher echelons of junior karting, £5,000 a year was being spent — it's £40,000 now — so I was paying for Johnny's racing; and he was racing every weekend and all over England.'

Bob says that 'in those days you were talking about a lot of money. People used to say *oh, Johnny's a sponsored driver* and that sort of thing, but it didn't involve being paid money. Bill couldn't afford that. He was a dealer and the only thing he could do was give Johnny a chance to race. There were fathers who had businesses and they could put their karting down to business expense. They were spending fortunes.'

Sisley, meanwhile, judges that Johnny 'was very shy, yes, angelic-looking, almost looked like a girl, really. He didn't talk to girls because they scared him — it wasn't that he didn't like them! His life was for racing — all he wanted to do was race, and his parents were completely committed. All their energies went behind Johnny's racing, although, because there was no money, essentially it was me subsidising it — but that certainly doesn't mean they weren't involved. It was very much a family effort. When he was younger Johnny was a most shy, reserved boy, not an intellectual. He'd had the minimal formal education as such. He didn't speak very well because his grammar wasn't good. He was interested in karting and nothing else, which is not unusual in kids.

'Even today there are kids whose dads and mums live and die karting and the only thing which matters is whether the son will become a motor racing driver or not. They are devoted to it and it's a national disaster if the son loses. Johnny's parents weren't like that totally, but they were committed to him doing well — they were completely behind him, and I'm sure they sacrificed everything for it. It must have cost Bob money, even going to meetings on a shoestring, but Johnny won the British Junior Championship, which is very difficult to do.'

Herbert left school at 14 with, as Sisley reiterates, 'no formal qualifications, and he started to work full time for us as a test driver.'

Bob explains that Johnny had already been 'helping Bill out working on karts' before he left school. 'It was our lives. We lived in a terraced house. I'd get home from work, come in through the front door, straight out through the back door into the garage every night to work on our karts. Anyone wanted me on the phone, we had an intercom. Don't forget we used to race every week, and all our money was channelled into racing.'

At 16 Herbert was, as a Buckmore Park brochure cryptically notes,

Action 1977, at Rye House. He's on the Tarantella (Herbert family).

'transferred to serve an apprenticeship with the Sisley Karting factory in New Romsey and became involved in manufacturing components and chassis for the race team. Unfortunately, however, his talents as a fabricator were a little less obvious than as a driver, and following production of "variable" shaft diameter stub axles, Johnny was soon put back into a kart!'

Or, as Sisley told me, 'Johnny was not a good engineer. He'd work for us in the factory helping out as well as developing the kart. We

Straight-line speed, 1978 (Herbert family).

were selling karts based on his success and selling so many we couldn't keep up — 500 a year all over the world. I had other drivers who contributed, but it was mainly because of Johnny. He was a glamour boy because of his exciting style, and people watched him because he was so naturally quick. He was a pure racer. If a kart had lost a wheel he'd still have driven it quickly on three! It didn't matter how badly the equipment was set up, how right or wrong we'd got it, he'd still be quick.

'As an example of his control, he could counter-balance a kart on two wheels, something I've never seen anyone else do — I'm told Roberto Moreno [a Formula 1 driver] could, but I never saw him. We had old-fashioned petrol pumps — we drew a figure of eight through and round these pumps, then Johnny would tip the kart on to two wheels and trace the figure. That takes so much skill because it ought to be impossible to balance a kart for that long. We had a stable of maybe ten quasi-works drivers and none of them could do it.'

In 1978 Johnny was selected to represent Great Britain in the Junior World Championships in Luxembourg. Bob explains that none of the family had ever been abroad before, even on holiday, 'but we had been to the Isle of Wight. We took our caravan to Luxembourg, towed it behind the car. We couldn't afford hotels. What did I think of Luxembourg as a country? You never saw anything — it was like going down to Tilbury: you arrived at the circuit, practised, raced, finish, home!

'When we went to World Championships we'd load up with the worn qualifying tyres that people had slung out and we'd use them back here to practice. Bill couldn't buy all these bits for testing, so we'd pick up these old tyres, mix 'n' match a set.'

Sisley gives a context. 'Up until two or three years ago the Italian-manufactured racing karts were the best and they were totally dominant. They were the gods of it, right? British drivers, although very skilful, never did any good in European racing because it was like playing football on a pitch you'd never seen before *and* with the wrong-sized boots *and* playing up a slope. The tyres were different, the whole thing was different. When we took Johnny to the Junior Worlds, which he did for us first of all, he had a disaster. He wasn't very quick at all. The Italians had special tyres and they used to cheat.'

Jane insists that 'people don't realise how professional it was. Qualifying engines . . .'

Bob insists that 'karting had *paper* tyres before Formula 1 had qualifying tyres. They lasted a lap and you threw them away. I don't know what they were, but I used to call them paper tyres because they didn't last. They'd leave them in their wrappers, carry the kart on to the grid, stand the kart on the wrappers then take them off. You'd do one very, very slow lap, your fast lap and the tyres were falling to pieces — if you were lucky you'd get your fast lap out of them.'

In time, Herbert drove a Polski Fiat on the roads and I asked Sisley what manner of driver he was. 'He was too quick. Not bad, mad . . .'

On the track he feared nobody. Bob explores that and explores the mystery of natural talent. 'The first thing he ever drove with gears was a 125cc kart. A chap called Geoff Page, who works for Brian Hart now [Hart, F1 engine manufacturer], raced 125s and we were at Fulbeck, Lincolnshire. Geoff's dad was always a great fan of Johnny's and he said *does Johnny want a little go at this?* We thought *oh — gears.* He went out and absolutely flew, and Geoff's old man couldn't believe it, couldn't believe how quick he was.

'John never worried about racing against anybody. When he first competed in internationals he was up against Terry Fullerton and there was always this myth about Fullerton [who Ayrton Senna rated the best driver he'd ever raced]. John simply went out and raced him. In fact, at their first meeting — John was just out of juniors — Fullerton was on the circuit timing him. Fullerton seemed a bit nervous. *There's a young kid out there flying round and he's going to give me a bit of a hard time.*'

In the autumn of 1982 Herbert competed in two events that represented, I suppose, the heights of the karting career. The first was at Fulbeck, and *Karting* magazine reported that 'in Heat 3 Herbert started to increase his lead by some ten lengths. With only five laps to go Richard Weatherley made a late charge but it was not enough to catch Herbert, who took the flag to win the first 135cc British Championship and become the youngest ever champion in the International class.'

The second was at Kalmar, Sweden, where Senna — then dominating Formula Ford 2000 single-seaters — returned to karts for a final attempt at the title that had always eluded him, the World

Bill Sisley and his team in 1980, Herbert middle (Bill Sisley).

Sisley in 1996, holding a team portrait (Author).

Championship. In free practice Herbert put in 'some good work' and was 18th after the Time Trials. In Heat 4 *Karting* reported that he was 'going great guns and after a minor bang with Ari Karhu (Finland) the new RAC 135cc Champion came home seventh.'

He lay 24th after the Heats and rose from 26th to 11th in the pre-Final.

'Herbert hitched up into seventh place' as the Final unfolded, but 'with less than two laps to go his hand went up as his chain snaked on to the track to sideline him.' He'd be classified 18th.

Sisley was 'importing Italian stuff and I managed to get Johnny a drive in a Birel, which was the top Italian kart, and he went to the Senior Worlds. He was very, very quick. To get as high as he did in the Final . . . well, for an English driver it was extremely good. I'll tell you how poor we were. We used to go round after the European meeting and keep the tyres that the Italians had thrown away — because they were better than the tyres we had when new [see Bob, above].

'Anyway, that was really the end of Johnny's karting career. He'd been working for me for a long time and he'd won everything he reasonably could. We had a unit at Brands Hatch where we made karts, and we let out the bottom half of this unit to a car manufacturer called Valour Racing. A man by the name of Paul Newman of Valour Racing walked in one day with his daughter, a young lady called Emily, and said he wanted her to become kart champion of the world. He said he had unlimited money and he was very plausible.

'Eventually he bought me out of the racing side of the kart business because he wanted to run it his own way to support his daughter's racing. Johnny worked for him. I had no contractual interest in Johnny, my interest in him was as a friend. Although I could have signed a contract with him [early on as a manager] and demanded 10 per cent of his earnings thereafter or whatever, I'm not interested in that. I'd helped him and he'd helped me.

'He had no money to go further, his dad couldn't afford it and he needed someone else's money behind him. I'd like to have sponsored him, but I didn't have the money either. And Valour Racing were there . . .'

To which Bob says: 'Paul Newman had taken over Bill's business and John used to help this girl. In karts she'd follow him around and he'd teach her the lines and everything else. He helped with the kart.

Preparing, racing, posing (Herbert family).

We never thought about single-seaters. Paul got John into car racing. I would never have got John into car racing, not because I wouldn't have wanted to but because of the money. It was completely out of my budget.'

I wonder if Sisley realised how good Herbert was. 'Yes. To my mind and as a rule of thumb, you have two types of kart driver who are successful: what I call the tactician, and what I call the racer. The tactician is always going to finish, and finish in the first two or three, but he's never going to win unless someone breaks down. He's very good technically, but he's not exciting to watch and he's not a racer. I like the racer type. Johnny comes under that category: the boy who will brake later than anyone else even though he might go off doing it. Kart racing is very fierce, and on the first lap of a race much fiercer than any other form of motor sport because there's 28 karts out there, they're all on cold tyres and you get lots of accidents.

Any kid who wins a British Karting Championship is good enough to make a racing driver

'The good driver will make up many places on the first lap. Any kid that I see who makes up ten places consistently against quality opposition is a very, very good racer. Then he has to be a good tactician after that. Any kid who wins a British Karting Championship is good enough to make a racing driver, and Johnny was bloody good. What I didn't know, because of his lack of money, was whether he'd go on and make it in cars. He needed a mentor to provide the means.'

Herbert made his racing car debut at the Brands Hatch Formula Ford Festival in 1983. The Festival always attracted a huge entry of 1600cc cars, and to do well in it, particularly to win it, might be important to the whole structure of a career. In Herbert's heat the magazine *Autosport* reported that a driver called John Oxborrow 'did a mighty job hauling his car back up to fourth place after being engulfed at the start, while perhaps more remarkable was the fifth position of karting graduate Johnny Herbert in a works Sparton. Herbert fought every inch of the way to inflict defeat on the experienced Wil Arif, Gary Knesevitch and Peter Bell.' He crashed when he was running tenth in his quarter-final.

In the final another Essex lad — a migrant from Stepney, actually — finished eighth. Perry McCarthy 'didn't know Johnny before the Festival, I didn't know his name either, hadn't heard of him. I can't even remember whether I spoke to him, but I don't think so. I remember seeing him because he was chatting to a bird I quite fancied. Mind you, I did beat him to that result.' Of all the drivers at the Festival, Herbert and McCarthy would become close friends. We shall see.

In 1984 Herbert embarked on what he thought would be a full season of Formula Ford 1600 racing with Valour. He drove the opening round of the BP 1600 Championship at Brands, finished sixth, and went testing at Oulton Park. 'I can remember turning into Old Hall [a right-hander] and overdoing it a bit,' he'd say. 'I kept my boot in and suddenly regained traction, but the car speared off to the right and flew into the barrier. I remember being dazed and trapped in the car. There was kind of a warm feeling in my leg but no real pain. I looked down and I remember thinking that one of the suspension links had torn my overalls. It was only when the rescue crew arrived and tried to move the car that I passed out. The thing had gone clean through my leg. In here and out there . . .'

Mike Baker, running a team called Racefax, was there 'testing with our driver Jonathan Bancroft — it was the days of Bancroft [regarded as very promising], Mark Blundell, those sort of people — and we all had to go out to help Johnny. He was trapped by the car's wishbone and semi-conscious. In the evening we went to see him at the hospital and he was a bit embarrassed because he'd had the wishbone embedded in his bum! For a year afterwards the wishbone hung in Valour's workshop with a caption about Johnny Herbert's bum. Anyway, that was the first time that I'd met him.'

McCarthy, meanwhile, 'only survived two races in '84, then I took off at Oulton Park and had a massive head-over-heels cartwheel accident and that put me out for virtually the whole year. During that year I started speaking to Johnny. We were from the same part of the world and by 1985 we were confirmed friends because he came to my engagement party. He was extremely shy, but once you got to know him he had a kind of warmth you'd respond to, because he is an open

31

man. He was reserved in the sense that a few of us were complete mad dogs — going out and creating havoc, loud mouths saying *we're the best* — and John didn't really get into all that. He could have just won the pools and he'd forget to tell you, honestly he would. If you asked if he'd had a good day he'd say *yeah, OK.'*

By July 1984 Herbert had regained his fitness and on 2 September won his first victory at Silverstone. *Autosport* reported that 'after a shambolic start, which saw poleman Blundell move left, forcing Andrew King into champion Bancroft's Reynard, the BP Superfind FF1600 round provided an excellent tussle for overall honours. While Blundell and Bancroft became immediate spectators, and the midfield men picked their way through a second incident at Copse, young Johnny Herbert (Valour Racing RF84) and the Monkey Lewis-run RF84 of Miles Johnston established themselves at the head of the field.

'Johnston slipped ahead on the second lap and a mighty tactical battle ensued as the pair outpaced the rest. Time after time Herbert led on to the Club straight only for Johnston to outbrake him, inside or out, into Woodcote. The turning point came on the penultimate lap when Miles overshot his turn-in point. Herbert capitalised, but Johnston was later on the brakes to reverse the order on the final corner. The wily Herbert kept his cool though, holding the tight line, and was just able to outdrag the Yorkshireman to the line.'

Although motor racing is a serious activity with potentially serious consequences, its lower reaches inevitably reflect such strange (to Formula 1) human characteristics as humour. For example, Baker remembers that Herbert's mechanic 'was a German guy called Alex Oxlinger — known as Hermann the German — who now works for Ford in Germany. There were some funny stories, like at Cadwell Park where Hermann opened the back of the transporter and the car almost rolled off — it was half hanging out of the back. He'd undone the straps before he realised that the paddock at Cadwell *sloped.* That's the way Hermann was. We all had to rush down and push the car back in! Another time Hermann took all the gauges out so he could paint little red arrows on them to make sure Johnny knew he couldn't go above those many revs . . .'

Right *Modest ambitions in the world of sponsorship* (Herbert family).

**Chloride Automotive
Batteries Limited**

Subsidiary of Chloride Group PLC

Registered Office
Chequers Lane
Dagenham. Essex
England RM9 6PX
Telephone 01-592 4560
Telex 261186
Cables Chloride Dagenham

Our ref.   JBN/sms/3073

Your ref.

Date   22nd November 1982

Mr J Herbert
46 Frinton Road
Collier Row
Romford
Essex

Dear Mr Herbert

Thank you for your letter of the 11th November and we would be
delighted to supply you with a battery for your caravan. However,
do you require a battery for lighting purposes or a battery for
starting purposes. If the former, then we could supply you with
our type 678 Portapower but if the latter we need to know what size
you require.

 We would supply this battery in exchange for a decal displayed
either on the kart or indeed on the caravan.

Looking forward to hearing from you.

I am,

Yours sincerely

J B NAYLOR
ADVERTISING & SALES PROMOTION MANAGER

Form No. OS. 016

CHLORIDE · DAGENITE · EXIDE
Registered in England. No 356617

Mike Langley worked for Valour, on the Formula 3 car of Ross Cheever (brother of Formula 1 driver Eddie). 'Then Johnny came and I helped on his car a little bit. What sort of a chap was he in those days? Well (chuckle), funny, like he is now, really, much the same but just younger, a bit scatter-brained. We used to send him to places to get parts and he'd go to the wrong place and all that. When he came back after the accident at Oulton, as a driver he got better and better, and by the time the Festival came you could see he was going to be flying.'

The 1984 Festival entry included Damon Hill, Eddie Irvine and an Austrian, Roland Ratzenberger. In the heats Herbert came second, which *Autosport* reported thus: 'Only the considerable talents of young Johnny Herbert kept him in touch with Gerrit van Kouwen for the first couple of laps, but the Valour Racing/Paul Newman-backed

From karts to Formula Ford 1600 with Valour (Herbert family).

34

lad did outstandingly well to hold off Ruairi O'Coileain's late charge.' Herbert was third in the quarter-finals, but in the semi-finals his 'fine run was sadly ended when the Valour car's throttle cable snapped as he started his fourth lap in sixth place.'

The heats at the Festival were always sponsored by different companies and Quest Racing had sponsored Herbert's. Quest Racing? Who? Thereby hangs a tale — of the immediate future.

• CHAPTER TWO •

Cheeky chappie

MIKE THOMPSON WAS a successful businessman with a company
that did sample surveys. He'd been a racing driver and had another
company — the very same Quest — that manufactured parts for cars.
Thompson is one of those interesting people who are imprecise about
some names and most dates, but very precise about all the essentials,
like what really happened and why.

'We must have originally met Johnny around 1983–84 because we
made wishbones for Valour. Johnny drove a Van Diemen and it was a
bit of a laugh because Johnny would always be going off circuits and
breaking the front left of the car. You'd come in, as it seemed, every
Monday morning and see an order for a front wishbone! I have a
vague memory of first meeting him in 1983. I saw him around. He'd
had the accident at Oulton with the wishbone in 1984 — when he
tried to get out and couldn't move — but I'd heard about him before
that.

'I've a private pilot's licence and the guy I share a plane with is
called Vic Gray whose son Terry karted with Johnny. In some of the
pictures, where they're all dressed up in their black leathers, you'll see
a tall guy and that was Terry. A very, very good driver. I do remember
Vic phoning me up one day and saying, "Johnny's a really good kid,
excellent kartist." So I'd heard about him. Anyway, I decided to

design a 1600cc racing car, which would be called the Quest, and we'd manufacture it. I didn't run the company on a day-to-day basis, however. A guy called Ian Blackman did that.'

Blackman, who, like Thompson, would now play a pivotal part in Herbert's career, was an old hand, as they say. 'I'd worked at Brands Hatch and, when I started, James Hunt was there as a pupil and Rupert Keegan [in Formula 1 from 1977 to 1982] was a pupil, too. I met Pete King and Ronnie Scott of the Ronnie Scott Jazz Club, and they did the Escort Mexico Championship. I continued for a few years with them, doing European touring cars — up to about 1980 — but then Pete had had enough.

'I decided to go into Formula Ford and set up a company doing race and engine preparation: we were running other people's Formula Fords — Van Diemens, Reynards, whatever. Mike Thompson was developing and building his own car, the Quest. We'd see him at the circuits fiddling around on his own, and I thought it would be nicer to have our own car rather than running all these big-make cars [which, in context, is what the Van Diemens and Reynards were]. I said to Mike, "Why don't we get together? We'll build your cars properly." And that's what we did.'

It was late 1984 and Quest, of course, needed something else: a driver.

'Nobody *with* money would drive a car *without* a proven background,' Blackman insists, 'whereas John wanted to drive and we had a car that we wanted *somebody* to drive!'

This method of selection, however, is never entirely straightforward, because the world is densely packed with impecunious teenagers anxious to drive anything; and, in fact, Thompson confesses that 'it wasn't me that decided to go with Johnny. We tested him and we tested another driver, Peter Rogers (who got killed in one of our cars two or three years later at Donington). *Peter* said he reckoned Johnny would be the one. All I really remember is that I went out in a car, and Johnny went out in a car, and he was bloody quick, especially in the entry to the corners where he made up a lot of his time.

'That was towards the end of 1984. Going into 1985 Ian selected him by saying he would be better than Peter. To be honest I think I was marginally in favour of Peter. Johnny was young and never looked fast, but he had an incredible ability to judge how much grip there was in a set of tyres. He could do that instantly, within a few corners, and the result was that, although he did not look fast, he was smooth, very, very smooth. Peter Rogers looked stunningly quick and on the day of the big test proved slightly quicker than Johnny, but Peter was more experienced. I believe Ian thought we could work better with Johnny although Peter was a lovely man and it was a fine call over who'd be best for us. Also Johnny had gone well in the Festival.'

(Incidentally, the impression of speed that a driver and car radiate can be an optical illusion. If a driver hurls a car at a circuit, digs smoke from the tyres under braking, has the back-end wobbling and sliding, if he thunders the kerbing, it gives a vivid impression of speed; but smoke and wobbles and slides all mean time lost. The ulti-mate fast lap is so controlled and so lacking in these dramas that you can be forgiven for missing it; but precious few human beings can create such a lap, simultaneously extracting the maximum from a racing car — raw, ravenous pace — *and* the minimum — placing it everywhere smoothly, easily and naturally.)

Blackman condenses the choice to these few words: 'We had vari-ous people driving but John was the main one. How did he strike me? Well, he *was* obviously talented, but everything was a bit of a joke, you know, fun. I don't think it was a serious thing for him in the beginning. Maybe in terms of a whole career he was too young to think what he was going to do, but he was obviously talented, obvi-ously he was good at it.'

Herbert had found the three dimensions he needed if the career was to continue — a car, the old hand to advise him what to do with it, and, in Thompson, the benefactor.

'Johnny never had any money,' Thompson says. 'He came down to the factory in Maidstone and worked and we paid him, gave him a bit, a pittance really. I'm not sure we even paid him in the orthodox sense — we gave him money when he needed it. He did deliveries, really, or whatever he could do to help — going to get bits, working on setting cars up, that sort of thing. You accept someone who hasn't any money because, at the end of the day, you think he's going to do some good for you. It's not totally altruistic. His actual contribution wasn't terri-bly high. Like any young kid he got bored easily and he did damage

Mike Thompson, the driving force behind Quest (Author).

the odd road car. He wrote off Ian's new Vauxhall that year . . .'

The team faced an immediate problem. 'We were not only trying to get John to do it, but trying to develop the car, an unknown quantity, to win races,' Blackman says. 'We knew John had the qualities and we hoped our car had the qualities. It was a question of combining them, but he was very inexperienced. That's where Mike helped. Mike was a driver and they did it between them. Mike did a lot of the testing.'

Blackman remains impressed by Herbert's attitude, and I sense that he thinks all racing drivers should be like this. 'Whatever we gave John, he did the best job he could with it. He'd get in and drive. He wouldn't stop half way and whinge *I can't drive this*. We worked from there.'

The factory was a new unit on a typical industrial estate, which is where you find almost every small and not so small team in the land. 'We had three works cars and we were selling cars around Europe, so we had lots of supplies and parts which needed moving around. That was John's job.' (To which Thompson adds: 'Johnny and another young chap, Gary Isles — who now races Nissan saloon cars — used to get up to all sorts of things. They'd go off in the van to collect stuff and they'd be driving down the motorway and they'd swap places while they were driving, as kids do . . .') As we have seen, in Britain there are usually several Formula Ford 1600 championships going on, and in 1985 Herbert would contest two, the Townsend Thoresen RAC and the Esso, with rounds of the European Championship to spice that.

He was in a car that was completely different from anything else

The RAC season began at Silverstone on 17 March. 'It was a great start. He was on pole position, I think, at Silverstone,' Thompson says — a trick of memory, although by no means a serious one in such a tight grid, Bancroft and Blundell on 1 minute 01.0, Paulo Carcasci (Brazil) on 1:01.2, Herbert and Bertrand Gachot on 1:01.3, Damon Hill on 1:01.7.

Autosport reported that 'a super start took Bancroft into an immediate lead, but the swarming pack made a fantastic sight as they swept down to Woodcote and the completion of lap 1. Gachot belied his lack of Silverstone experience by reaching as high as second place on the all-important final lap, but young Johnny Herbert timed his run to perfection and brilliantly outbraked the Belgian into Woodcote.'

Thompson guards fragments of memory. He says that Blundell, who'd made a bad start and recovered, 'caught Johnny up and Johnny got a bit of elbow.' Elbow? 'Well, Johnny was a bit nervous, you know, tightened up a bit, like people can do.' Whatever, Blundell got the Woodcote chicane all wrong on lap 10 of the 12 and it finished

Bancroft	12:27.9
Herbert	12:28.6
Gachot	12:28.8
Blundell	12:30.1

'We were to have a really good year,' Thompson says. 'We were one car against a field of Van Diemens. Johnny was always there or thereabouts. He was also in a car that was completely different from

40

anything else. I always designed them a bit weird — for instance, they didn't have any roll bars — so it wasn't the easiest car to get used to; but it was a car which suited him ultimately, because it had a lot more grip than other Formula Fords. However, you can scrub off speed if you have too much grip, and that's what tended to happen. It was funny sort of problems with the car.'

At the third round — Silverstone, 8 April — *Autosport* reported that 'Hill and Blundell ran wide of another scrap going on, with Damon assaulting the back of Herbert's Quest, which had been a strong second until finding itself in the catch fencing as a result.'

And thereby hangs another tale. 'Coming to the chicane,' Thompson says, 'Johnny braked early, the field engulfed him and he got knocked off. I put my arm around him back at the pits and I said — it was a joke for ever after that — *butcher's apron!* I said, "Johnny, you've really got to decide if you want to do this, because if you don't hack motor racing there is nothing else you can do." His mind was racing. I added, "Well, the only other thing you can do is be a butcher's assistant." And it was the joke from then on. *Butcher's apron.*'

'Cadwell Park, the next race, was interesting because we were constantly developing the car and I'd designed some new uprights for it. I thought they were fabulous, incredibly light. I was standing with Ralph Firmin [of Van Diemen] where the bump is. Johnny came round, went over the bump and the upright collapsed. I'll never forget the look on old man Firmin's face as Johnny came limping to a halt at our feet with all the car steaming [meaning *you designed this, Mr Thompson?*]. That evening we strengthened them so he was able to compete in the race; but he had these sorts of problems to contend with, the car being developed, and as I said the car was a bit weird.

'We had an advertising campaign going on in *Autosport*. We'd put these adverts in which Ralph Firmin used to get very upset about. I think it was at Thruxton that Johnny was hit by Carcasci [a works Van Dieman driver] and our advert said something like

GOT POLE POSITION BUT WAS ASSAULTED
FROM BEHIND BY A BRAZILIAN WITH V. D.

'*Autosport* put it in — we had a lot of those adverts during the year and, yes, Ralph got upset . . .'

On 14 July, in the EFDA Euroseries round 2 at Brands Hatch, Herbert took pole (from Hill), made a crisp start and was not to be caught. It was the first car win of his career and, in context, hadn't been long in coming.

I sought an evaluation from Mike Langley, who'd joined Quest. 'Johnny was very good in cars very quickly. You could see straight away that he was a natural driver. He didn't have to try very hard, you know. The set-up of a car? He wouldn't have any idea what was going on at all, he'd just get in and drive — and that was it. He was very tidy — he always looked like he was two-tenths off the pace, and yet he was *on* the pace. You'd stand and watch him at places like Paddock (at Brands) and you'd think *come on John, get on with it.* Then, when you saw his lap times, they were the sort of times everybody else should have been doing. In a sense it could be almost frustrating to watch: you'd be thinking about how he ought to be getting on with it, and really he was, but it simply didn't look like that.' The optical illusion, in fact.

I sought an evaluation from Ian Blackman. 'It was always serious for us as a team, but it can be difficult for a young kid, who is doing something that somebody else is paying for, to be totally serious. It's difficult to say what I'm saying. We'd known Senna in Formula Ford 1600 (in 1980) and he was totally serious. I ran Ross Cheever and he was, too. Ross was a bit of a prima donna, his whole life concentrated on Formula Ford — because he wanted to do well and go on to Formula 1 or whatever. There was no other conversation, *nothing* else, and when he turned up at the circuit he was in a tunnel. John's not like that at all. It was fun. When he got in the car he did the job, but apart from that there was never any deep concentration.'

How did he take the wins, the poles?

'Well, that's what we expected him to do. We did push him, we wanted him to do well, but *he* wanted to do well.'

How do you push a driver?

'Well, we used to beat him.'

What do you mean, beat him?

'Fight him. Give him a hard time. John was reasonably consistent, but again it was difficult because we, as a car manufacturer, weren't as consistent as he was. We were giving him something different all the time.'

Herbert easing himself into the Quest (Herbert family).

I sought an evaluation from Perry McCarthy. 'I noticed something in 1985, although I'd seen a bit of it the year before. Johnny races within a *family* or makes the team his family. He operates in environments where people generally warm to him and like him; and he gets the best out of everybody because of his talent. The team has gelled and warmed around Johnny and that's the environment he either creates or likes to be in. It's the same with all of us. That's what we'd all like, but he's certainly had it on a fairly consistent basis. He had it with Sisley, he had it with Thompson, and in the future he'd find it again.'

A round of the Esso Championship at Silverstone offers several insights into the developing career. *Autosport* reported that 'from fifth over the line on completion of lap 1, Herbert had the Quest up to third by lap 5, and this became second as he slipstreamed past Blundell into Stowe [Damon Hill leading]. Blundell was back ahead next time round, having set a new lap record, but Herbert bettered the mark to reclaim the place on the very next lap. Not to be outdone, Mark stormed ahead again on the eighth tour with yet another record.'

Into the final lap Hill still led, 'driving like a Silverstone veteran, protecting the inside line into the chicane for the final time. At least he thought he was, until his mirror revealed Herbert barrelling down the grass on his right. Johnny realised he wasn't going to make it and flicked left to give himself a quicker line through the chicane. Across the line they shot as near to a dead heat as was possible. Herbert thought he had got up on the line, but on the timing beam Hill was 0.001 secs up. Herbert and the Quest team originally appealed against the decision, but withdrew the protest and accepted the decision with smiles and good humour.'

Thompson remembers that 'Johnny's dad was there. Johnny and Damon went over the line virtually together but Damon won. His dad came up — his dad was always a big rule man — and asked me to protest. That was something that I hated and tended not to do. He said, "I was in the commentary box and I heard Tiff Needell say to Murray Walker that John definitely won the race and that we should protest." So I put in a protest as much to humour his dad as anything. Nightmare. I mean, how often do you protest and win because they've got it wrong on the line? His dad said he wanted them to see a replay of the television . . .'

Blackman confides that 'we tried to keep his dad away from some of the races. We all tried to push John, but his dad pushed him harder than we did. Some of the times at the races, we felt, it would cause a bigger distraction than it did good. Protests? That was from karting, which is a different world. They want to protest everything and fight everybody! It's madness, isn't it? We had to be a bit diplomatic with his dad, and it didn't really work, anyway, because his dad and mum always used to come. They had a caravan and they'd come along. There were the odd occasions at faraway tracks like Oulton Park where they wouldn't — but our suggestions didn't really work . . .'

If 1985 wasn't triumph after triumph, Herbert made solid progress, and now one event remained, the Festival at Brands. A couple of weeks before it Quest invited Marcus Pye of *Autosport* to test drive the car round Brands. 'Throw it over the kerbs,' they instructed, 'and then see what happens' — something usually inviting disaster in an FF1600. Pye, an experienced driver, did as he was bidden and found to his amazement there was some device on the car that kept it stable. Pye believes that this device might not have been invaluable at every circuit, but certainly was at kerb-clad Brands; and this played its part in what happened next.

Meanwhile, Thompson's naughty campaign against the Van Diemens continued with this advertisement in Pye's organ:

JOIN THE FIGHT AGAINST V. D.
Buy a Quest!

Unit 9, Wren Industrial Estate,
Coldred Road, Parkwood
Maidstone, Kent.

The Festival was over the Friday, Saturday and Sunday, with Friday

Ian Blackman — with a Caterham 7 in 1996. He guided Herbert at Quest (Author).

practice from 7.30 to 10.05 am — but not for Herbert. *Autosport* reported that 'the blond figure stalked back to the paddock, helmet in hand, face contorted in frustration and sheer disbelief. Once, twice, he buried his fist into the helmet. Herbert had planted his Quest, the much-fancied Festival winner, into the fence on his very first lap of qualifying and sentenced himself to the back of the grid with a 10-second penalty for the first heat.'

It's a major legend in the Festival and a bit of a minor legend in British motor sport generally; not more but certainly not less. Incidentally, to qualify you had to do three laps. If you didn't, and Herbert hadn't, you could take part in the race, but — as the report said — from the back and with a 10-second penalty.

The first witness to the legend is Thompson. 'Brands Hatch? Obviously he stuffed it. He ran back to the pits and we were wetting ourselves laughing! The car was so bloody quick, and then come the day, second lap he got off on dust. It happened half way round Paddock Bend. He braked a bit late or something, got it sideways or maybe something broke — we never established what happened, and he wasn't sure. *I* think it was dust because I remember it was dusty that day. We had to repair the car, but the whole team had lavished so much time on it during the season that we knew everything about it, and Ian was very good at it.'

The second witness is Mike Langley. 'We welded the gearbox and all that business. We'd transported it back to the Valour workshop [at the circuit] and it took an hour or so to fix. Johnny handled the Festival really well after that. Thompson had a little chat with him (chuckle) about it, you know, a bit of abuse for shunting it so early.' *Butcher's apron?* 'We thought it was amusing because of how Johnny went, "Oh well, I'll just have to get on with it, I'll just have to try harder tomorrow." I think that was partly because he knew he was good. He had a lot of self-belief. The people who are good don't have to keep telling you about it — no, they just get on with it . . .'

Herbert had to come from the back, of course. *Autosport* reported that the first heat 'stretched out into just the sort that Herbert did not want, with no one battling with anyone else [ie holding each other up]. Herbert's progress was, however, startling, and by lap 6 he was up to tenth. By lap 7 he was eighth and up against Kevin Gillen. The Sealink-backed driver gave no ground to Johnny and it seemed as though the Quest driver might come unstuck, but perseverance paid and they both made it by Ted Whitbourn before Johnny took Kevin.' That was sixth.

In the quarter-finals he started from the middle of the fifth row and needed a good finish to secure a place near the front of the grid for the semi-finals. Because the cars formed up 3–2–3–2–3, there were in effect ten cars in front of Herbert for the quarter-final. At the green he went to the outside for Paddock and remained outside up to Druids. On the brief descent from there he was ninth, and across the remainder of the lap overtook two cars to be seventh. From there he moved past Eric van de Poele (who'd reach Formula 1) for sixth, and by lap 4 was fifth. Two laps later he took Andy King — fourth. Now he pursued Allan Seedhouse, and in catching him broke the lap record. Herbert couldn't pass, and he and Seedhouse were both recorded at 10:02 crossing the line.

The car at Brands was stunning and it suited Johnny's style perfectly

He began his semi-final in the middle of the third row, knowing that the first 13 of the 26 starters would reach the final. At the green Gachot — middle of the front row — was touched by another car and somersaulted, rolling across and partially down Paddock, stopping the race and eliminating four cars. At the re-start Herbert took the outside line round Druids again. It gave him the inside line for the next corner, a left, and he ran fourth. He tracked Seedhouse, pressured him, slotted inside, took him: clean, concise, classical.

He began to catch Bancroft (leading) and O'Coileain and did another 48-second lap. At Paddock he tried the outside, but O'Coileain resisted, the cars side by side. On lap 11 at Surtees, the uphill left leading out into the country, O'Coileain got sideways, seemed to have caught it, hadn't, ploughed off on to the grass. Herbert was through. He closed on Bancroft, pressured him, darted and probed and was still probing as they crossed the line. Both were timed at 12:33.

Damon Hill won the other semi-final, incidentally.

Herbert had the left-hand position on the front row for the final.

At this green — although fractionally slower on to the power than Hill — he had enough momentum by Paddock to lead, Bancroft second, Hill third. The Festival was decided, no matter that mid-way through the 20 laps Bancroft was very close and menacing. Herbert confessed that he'd 'eased up a bit too much', accelerated and that was that.

'Johnny started from the back and he did it really well, he didn't go mad,' Thompson says. 'Come the final, he just did a perfect race. You know Ronnie Scott's Club? Pete King co-owns it, and he was a bene-factor in those days. He helped the team a lot — he was a great fan of Johnny's and he was there that day. He was extremely enthusiastic. After Johnny had won, Pete was running down the pit lane. We'd

Mark Blundell, the competitor (Tyrrell Yamaha).

gone to scrutineering. The scrutineer checked the car, fine, no problem, walked out, knew Pete and saw Pete coming. Just as they passed,
the scrutineer [very naughtily] shook his head and [very naughtily]
said *all lost for 2lbs in weight*. *Absolutely ridiculous*. Pete came rushing
over and I though he was going to have a heart attack!

'The car at Brands was stunning and it suited Johnny's style
perfectly. If you speak to Adrian Reynard he reckons he's never met
anyone able to suss out a set of tyres as well as Johnny, how much grip
and so on. It's a gift to be able to do that, but it's also starting young.
In karting they were on to one-lap qualifying tyres when he was 13,
14, so you get into that very, very quickly. Whatever racing you do
it's useful experience, but in karting in particular you have to spend a
lot of time getting the kart right, and this question of grip is v-e-r-y
important. Great training.'

How did Herbert take the win?

'Johnny is very fatalistic. *What will be will be* is Johnny's basic make
up, and he takes things in his stride. He wasn't fazed by it, but obviously he was really chuffed. I think he likes racing. He doesn't necessarily like being in a car going round and round and round — he likes
competing, winning. He never enjoyed testing. Whatever formula he
was in he didn't like the testing. That held him back a little bit
because certainly from Formula 3 upwards you've got to get the car
together, got to work on that.

'In Formula 1 at Lotus with Mika Hakkinen in 1992 is an example
of this fatalistic approach. First part of that year Johnny tended to
out-qualify him, second part Hakkinen tended to out-qualify Johnny.
Hakkinen would pore over the telemetry, he'd be there till 10 o'clock
at night. Johnny wasn't into that. It's not because he didn't have the
intellect — he gives the impression of not being particularly bright,
but he is. I used to play chess with him a lot — he was quite good, but
he couldn't really focus his attention on it. To him, it was as if it was
a car: you get in it and it either works for you or it doesn't. He
enjoyed playing chess when we flew to the Grands Prix. It's a game
you've got to concentrate on, and concentration wasn't his biggest
asset in motor racing — because he wanted to get on with it.

'I remember Peter Collins saying he was really impressed with
Johnny's attitude when he won the Festival because Johnny took it in
his stride.'

Peter Collins did not forget.

Perry McCarthy gives a racer's context. 'Personally I don't get carried away by winning or coming second or third. I'm pleased, I'm happy, but it's the people around you who are coming up and kissing you and hoisting you aloft and everything else. That is nice for them. Like me, Johnny expects to win. When success comes you think *that's good*, and if success is sustained it dilutes your emotions even more. In this sport, winning is the easiest thing to understand. Anything other than winning demands explanations. That said, to win the Festival was fantastic — and fantastic for me, watching a mate win it.'

Shortly afterwards Herbert was given a run by a team called Pegasus in their Formula 3 car. He covered 130 laps of the Silverstone club circuit, using wet tyres in the morning on a damp track, slicks in the afternoon.

Pegasus team manager Trevor Foster was quoted as saying, 'We were amazed at the way Johnny took to the car, and the formula, so quickly. He was excellent to work with, understood what he was doing and was not overawed. He didn't put a foot wrong — no damage, no missed gears, no moments. His commitment was 100 per cent. One would have thought this was Herbert's fifth or sixth Formula 3 test, not his first. He's certainly capable of moving straight into the formula on this form.'

His best time, 54.2, would have put him on the front row for the Marlboro British F3 round at the circuit in August.

These many years later, Foster confirms that this is exactly what he said and felt. 'Pegasus had run an English driver, Andrew Gilbert-Scott, in 1983 and he'd won the Festival. One of the Pegasus sponsors was a sponsor at the Festival, and we had moved into Formula 3, so I thought it would be a nice idea not only to stay a Festival sponsor but offer a test day to the winner. It just happened that in 1985 that was Johnny Herbert. I didn't really know him at all, although I'd noticed him, as you do. You pick up the odd report here and there, and I'd seen him race a couple of times. He was having a difficult time with very little sponsorship and racing a Quest.

'He came along. He struck me as very laid-back, very easy-going, took it all in his stride. It was a typical Silverstone club test day, a Friday I think, and he did a very good job. He adapted his style to suit the car and drove and drove and drove. We'd gone through the whole car explaining it to him, and we tried changing it a bit because he felt he was losing time at Becketts, but without "hurting" the car somewhere else [making it slower there] it was very difficult to do that. He said, "Oh, don't worry, I'll adapt to that," and off he went.'

Bob Herbert remembers that 'when John got home I asked him how many laps he'd done and he said *about 40 or something*. He was really taken aback because each time he came in to the pits he'd say something, Trevor twiddled, he'd go faster, come in again, Trevor twiddled, he'd go faster . . .'

> ## You would expect Johnny to be quick.
> ## He has innate car control

For the first time in his career, Herbert was experiencing a car that was sophisticated enough to have permutations and adjustments.

Foster says that 'there is no doubt in my mind that naturally talented drivers can jump up a formula and make cars go fast straight away. Because of Johnny's ability, I personally believe that if I had been running a Formula 3000 team I could have put him in it that day and he'd have done a similarly exceptional job. I've worked with a lot of drivers over 20-plus years and I really do believe you can make a competent driver.

'Take a Joe Bloggs off the street, for argument's sake. Providing he has a reasonable amount of co-ordination, can drive his road car, has enough willpower and enough money, over time you can make him a reasonably good racing driver. He goes round and round, crashes the car, you put it back together again, he goes round and round, crashes the car, you put it back together again . . .

'Then he goes racing and when he's mastered Formula Ford he goes up to Formula 3 and so on; but he will never be stunning in any formula. He can reach a competent level and there is no great magic to that, although it will take longer than if the driver had natural talent, which was Johnny's case. What makes the difference is the fact that you can take the very, very talented — like Johnny — out of the formula they are in, give them something to drive with twice the power and twice the weight, and within five or ten laps they're saying *well, it feels a bit flat actually, it doesn't seem to be very punchy out of the corners*.'

McCarthy wasn't surprised at Herbert's speed. 'You would expect Johnny to be quick. He has innate car control, he doesn't worry and he doesn't psyche himself out. I've always felt there aren't as many filter systems in his decision-making process as there are with many other people. From being a *thought* it goes to his feet and that's it, he just does it. He has always been a very natural driver.

'I think of drivers in terms of a pie-chart [a circle carved into different percentage 'slices']. You can have different drivers all coming up 100%, but the chart is made up of characteristics — they can be determination, fitness, innate ability, technical feedback, confidence, all manner of things — which come up 100%. A large portion of Johnny's pie chart is sheer, natural talent. There weren't that many drivers about who I really, really asked myself *are they as good as me or are they better than me?* Johnny was someone I looked at big time, and also Martin Donnelly and occasionally Julian Bailey.'

'It was a great chance at the end of the season,' Herbert said of the test, 'and brilliant to be back on slicks [since the karting days — FF 1600s had all-weather tyres]. Apart from the fantastic grip I found I was able to judge the Formula 3 car's limits so much more easily, and once I got used to the incredible braking I could turn into corners and stand on the power straight away. I'm very grateful to Pegasus for their testing offer, which has made me even keener to race in Formula 3 as soon as possible.'

Autosport commented: 'Johnny's immediate plans are to develop Quest's first Formula Ford 2000 chassis, to be launched at the London Racing Car Show in January. Mike Thompson's team, which gave him his big break in FF1600 this season, will field a works car for him in 1986. Unless an F3 budget intervenes?'

'The second year,' Blackman says, 'we did Formula 2000. He had just won the Festival, but so had Quest, which meant it wasn't only John who had made his mark. We had, too. We started to get busy, more people wanting to buy our cars. For this second year John couldn't do Formula Ford 1600 again because if you're serious about making progress you don't do it twice when you've been successful at it. He had to move on, but he still had no money — there wasn't a penny. As a team, the *logical* move for us was 2000 — because it was

Right *The way we were. Some interesting names at Brands in 1985.*

BRITISH RACING
AND SPORTS CAR CLUB

FAILSAFE BATTLE OF BRANDS SPORTS CAR INTERNATIONAL
BRANDS HATCH CIRCUIT
SATURDAY/MONDAY 24th/26th AUGUST 1985

INFORMATION SHEET NO: 10

WEATHER CONDITIONS: Sunny, Track Dry   TIME PUBLISHED: 11.05

RAC/TOWNSEND THORESEN FORMULA FORD 1600 PRACTICE

NO	DRIVER	TIME
8	Mark Blundell	49.21
1	Ruairi O'Coileain	49.43
6	Johnny Herbert	49.47
7	Jonathan Bancroft	49.50
16	Jeremy Packer	49.52
9	Bertrand Gachot	49.59
45	Paulo Carcasci	49.59
22	Perry McCarthy	49.73
23	Tim A Jones	49.74
64	Peter Rogers	49.82
12	Alexander Arbis	49.89
10	Lindoro Da Silva	49.92
18	Phillippe Favre	49.97
5	Damon Hill	50.25
48	Kevin Gillan	50.73
20	Nicky D'Amico	50.74
14	Eddie Ervine	51.19
15	Bob Bailey	52.01

AMENDMENT TO INFORMATION SHEET NO 9

The driver of car No 48 should have been listed as Duncan Bain and NOT Mike Catlow

CARS NOT SEEN: 21   Greg Hart

another route for us to sell cars. We thought, 'Let's put him in a 2000 car and see if he can do it again.'

Thompson reinforces that. 'Year two, 2000. Why? Money, really. We were making cars for 2000 and Johnny couldn't get a Formula 3 drive. The way in those days was to go 2000, a fairly common route. I designed the car again, but it was a "brick" really, never worked and to this day we don't know why.

'He had some good results and stuck at it. I always used that as an example to other drivers if they'd say a car was useless. Stick at it. Johnny never moaned. That's the fatalism again, and it works both ways because Johnny is very good in those situations: no moaning and groaning and so on. *If it happens, it happens.* If he has a crash or finishes 13th he'll be trying to the last moment, and that is such a good thing for a team — you knew he was a constant. Once he'd got over the early tightening up in 1600 he was not a variable. He gave 100% and gave it all the time. From a designer's point of view that's excellent. He did well with the car, really . . .'

As far as I was concerned he was going to Formula 1

Blackman accepts that 'the problem was that the car wasn't as successful as the Formula Ford. Johnny did a better job, if you like, in that the car was worse and he still did reasonably well. The other side of it was that we, also, had no money, and it costs a lot to develop a new car. It's not cheap. How did he take all this? In his stride, because he felt we were trying to do the best for him. If that was the best we could do for him, he was happy to accept it — plus he'd got a drive. That's how I felt he saw it: we kept him driving and we kept him on the scene so people could see what he was doing. After he'd won the Festival we thought eventually Formula 1.'

Whatever the logic and attractions of 2000, the next important step would have to be Formula 3, and Thompson was 'keen for him to get into that because as far as I was concerned he was going to Formula 1, and in 1986 he did some races for an F3 team.' That team, Mike Rowe Racing, gave Herbert his debut at Donington on 20 July.

Autosport reported that he was 'sensational, the young Romford driver qualifying seventh. Herbert attacked both circuit and challenge with gusto — and considerable skill from the outset, it must be said. Quickest of all in the early minutes, Johnny wound up fifth at the break, having nudged the nose-cone at McLeans.' He finished fifth in the race.

Trevor Foster had left Pegasus and joined another Formula 3 team, Swallow, and 'I tried very much to get Johnny in the car, but it was the same old story, sponsorship not available. Then he found some money and ran with Mike Rowe. I was at Donington. The owner of Swallow Racing was a guy called Tim Stakes, and I keep a categorical memory of having a bet with him. We were talking about Herbert — because I'd insisted he's the guy to watch and I'd raved about him from that test day with Pegasus — and I said *bet you any money he'll qualify in the top eight*. I'm not normally a gambling man, and I can't recall how much the amount was — £10 or whatever. Tim said *no, no, he'll never do that*. I said *I think you'll be surprised*. Johnny was right up there the whole time at Donington in a car being run with a low budget. He did a blinding job.'

McCarthy remembers that 'when Johnny first came into Formula 3 — and we used to smile about it — the family environment happened: they'd put their arms around Johnny all the time as if he was a five-year-old and they were showing him round the pits!' He'd do another six races, including a British round at Zolder, Belgium, because traditionally the British Championship embraced rounds on the near-Continent. Thompson says that 'the whole team — about five of us — stayed in a bloody caravan in the paddock. Race morning was perfect silence except the birds singing. It was Johnny's turn to do breakfast. About seven in the morning it was so quiet you could hear him cooking. He had a bit of a cold, and he made this enormous sneeze and you heard the pan sizzle because he'd just sneezed into it. Everyone killed themselves laughing. It took us about an hour to recover. The sneeze summed up the weekend — it wasn't the most successful.' Herbert was tenth.

He'd done well enough in Formula 3 to be noticed by Eddie Jordan, but, as Thompson points out, Herbert 'needed benefactors to do racing right from FF1600 onwards. We did say to Eddie that Johnny didn't have any money. It wasn't our team, we didn't make the cars, so we had to raise the money. Eddie's budget was £120,000 for the season in Formula 3, which we did raise. We found it, paid every penny and paid it on time. We had a good relationship with Eddie that year, very good.

'It was brilliant for Eddie because — and this is going back to Johnny's testing thing [or rather his dislike of it] — Johnny would go to a circuit and do, say, 15 laps. Sometimes it would be on the pace, sometimes it wouldn't, but he'd say *that'll be fine for the race* and it was. You know what Formula 3 is usually like. They pound round all bloody day and put their times in at the end. From Eddie's point of view, to have someone who could hack it without doing miles of test-ing — well, Eddie loved it, brilliant. The amount of expense he had that year was much, much lower. It was a strong field in 1987 and Eddie had a very good engine, which helps a lot, but Johnny just did it perfectly.'

In fact, after the Donington debut Foster 'spent the rest of 1986 trying to persuade Tim Stakes and Swallow to sign Johnny up for 1987. We did have a meeting with Johnny, but for some reason — I don't know why — I couldn't get Tim to dip into his pocket for Johnny Herbert, which was a mistake. We did talk to him, he'd got a little bit of money, we tried to make it happen, and in the end he decided to go to Eddie. Having said all that, he won the champion-ship, so you can't say he made a mistake.'

Eddie Jordan has exercised a formative influence on many young drivers. He formed his own team in a lock-up garage at Silverstone in 1980, retired as a driver and devoted himself to running it and managing young drivers. In 1983, 1984 and 1986 a Jordan driver finished second in the British Formula 3 Championship. Herbert was about to change all that, and set the tone immediately, taking pole at the first round — Thruxton, 15 March — with a lap of 1:11.50. That compared with the next best of 1:12.64 by a Dutchman, Peter Kox. Herbert made a bad start but surged into the lead by overtaking Gachot, who said, 'He was in a different race. I saw the speed he caught me and we were not yet at half distance. If I had blocked him, for sure we would both have been off. I was happy to let him go.'

McCarthy insists that it was 'obvious from Johnny's few outings in Formula 3 the year before that he was going to be a substantial chal-lenger for the championship. Jordan had a development-tuned Volkswagen engine. I still tease Johnny and he teases me about that

Peter Collins — far right and in Lotus days — kept a careful eye on Herbert (second left) and gave him a test with Benetton (Lotus).

season because I am convinced he had an engine advantage, certainly over me. I was particularly unhappy, but if anybody was going to beat me I wanted it to be Johnny.

'Straight away he was into the *family* atmosphere again. You could see, by the way he got on, that it was going to be home for him. By this time he'd moved to within one mile of my place in Essex, so we saw each other literally every day of the week. He'd come home for dinner, we'd go training together, have a laugh and so on and so forth. It's unusual two people competing in different teams doing that, but we just hit it off.

'I was mad dog to his calm approach. I liked the calmer bit and he probably liked the mad dog bit! We knocked around everywhere and raced down country lanes, and we'd see what new *attitude* we could bring the car into the drive at home without wiping out the kids who were playing on the lawn. We were very, very close.

'One of Johnny's remarkable assets is this. Here I am, Perry

McCarthy, somewhat hard-headed and racing *against* him — somebody who is actually in a better position than me, and is certainly getting better results than I am — and there were times when I wanted to help him! I've never really worked out why that was. My dad knew Johnny, would put his arm round him and say, "How you doing, son?" Then he'd look at me and Julian Bailey and say, "Well, you pair of bastards can make your own way in life, but we've got to look after John." I think it was because he was little and had long blond hair, which I am pleased to say has started to go. That's great, I tell you. I can't wait. Every time I see a picture of him I study it to see how far back it's gone. If it's another half an inch I call him up and say, 'It's going, it's going, and I'll be there when it's gone . . .'

By Monaco and the traditional support race to the Grand Prix — 30 May — Herbert had competed in seven rounds and won four of them. He had 50 points, Gachot 32, Gary Brabham 24, with Damon Hill eighth on 8. At Monaco Herbert would meet such as Jean Alesi, Nicola Larini and a talented 'local' Frenchman called Didier Artzet (he came from Nice). Herbert qualified fourth and finished third behind Artzet and Alesi, the best performance by a Briton since 1984, when James Weaver came third.

By September Herbert could secure the championship — at Spa — but, before he went there, he was given a drive at Brands Hatch in the Formula 1 Benetton, a team then run by Peter Collins. It was otherwise an ordinary test day at the circuit with several teams there.

Bob Herbert '*had* to take a day off work. I was just about self-employed, so I could.' He and Jane positioned themselves between the two grandstands opposite the pits but 'we didn't actually go to the pits. Mansell was *lolling* around over everybody, all you could hear from Derek Warwick's garage was laughter, Senna was obviously very serious. I remember a great big group of people also standing around where we were. Johnny was wearing a plain white helmet and some of the people were asking *who's that in that helmet?* and others said *it's Johnny Herbert* — because there are always some people who know what's going on. We didn't say anything, then we moved down to Clearways.'

In fact it was a gathering.

Blackman: 'He got the drive and obviously we all went to Brands for that day. Here was this young boy, because that's all he was, and

Formula 3 action, vintage 1986 (Formula One Pictures).

Formula 3 action, vintage 1987 (Formula One Pictures).

somehow it seemed as if he was going to a fairground, not to drive a Formula 1 car! The mood was *phoo, this is the business.* Benetton had one of their regular drivers there [Thierry Boutsen, who'd been in F1 since 1983]. The car was a turbo, of course, and John had never sat in anything like that. He ended up as quick as the other driver! We were all standing at Clearways and he'd be coming through with the thing sideways waving from the cockpit at us.

'It didn't surprise me that he could do this. I expected him to. For instance, at that time no way would you ever think Damon Hill would make Formula 3000, let alone Formula 1. He wasn't in the same league as Johnny. Definitely not Eddie Irvine, either. They were just there, that's all, they were constantly having crashes and they seemed to be driving above their ability.'

Thompson: 'It was on the Indy circuit, and through Clearways third lap he was already doing a good time, waving to his mum and dad. Johnny was stunning.'

Bob Herbert: 'I had a video camera and I shot some film and it shows more of the grass than Johnny because I was absolutely astonished — I was swinging this video camera around instead of using it properly! I just couldn't believe the speed. Mike was clocking him, Ian was clocking him, and the conversation would go *Johnny's done a so-and-so* and then *no, he can't have done.* I think he was only three-tenths off Mansell's time.'

Jane: 'The point was, it was a tighter circuit than the full Grand Prix one, and other Formula 1 drivers were there. He hadn't been given an empty circuit somewhere to go round by himself getting used to it all. He had to be aware of everybody else.'

Sisley: 'I saw the Benetton test and he was flying, absolutely magical.'

Autosport: 'Despite using Boutsen's seat, and thus not being as comfortable in the car as he would have liked, Herbert scorched round the 1.2-mile Indy circuit in 36.4 sec, some 0.3 sec quicker than Boutsen managed, although the Belgian was out at a different time of the day. Herbert's performance caused quite a stir, apparently being just 0.2 from the mark set by Ayrton Senna's Lotus-Honda. Nigel

Right *Award winner in Formula 3. That's Martin Donnelly in the Benetton* (Herbert family).

Mansell topped the day with a best of 34.99. Herbert himself was typically modest in appraising his performance. "I think I did OK but I could probably have done a better job if I had been for a proper seat fitting.'" Then he departed for Belgium.

'I got to Spa,' McCarthy says, 'and remember I used to see Johnny every day, he's at ours for dinner, etc, etc. So I was at Spa, I'm looking round for him and I can't see him anywhere. Where the bloody hell is he?'

McCarthy asked someone, who replied, 'He'll be here shortly. He's been delayed because of his test at Brands.'

'WHAT TEST AT BRANDS?'

'He's been put in a Benetton.'

'NO HE HASN'T!'

'He-has-been-out-in-a-Benetton and — he went quicker than Boutsen.'

'Do me a favour and shut up.'

'Honestly.'

'Listen, stop winding me up, will you?'

When Herbert did arrive, McCarthy tackled him head on to clear up this nonsensical fiction of Benetton, Boutsen and Brands. 'That *do-do* over there reckons you were in a Benetton and you were quicker than Boutsen,' quoth McCarthy.

'I was.'

McCarthy looked at him and said, 'I DO NOT BELIEVE YOU — I believe you were there, but I do not believe you didn't tell me.' Herbert replied, 'It all happened too late in the day, I had to go and that was it. There was no chance to tell you.'

Now, at Spa and concentrating on the Formula 3, *Autosport* reported that 'Johnny Herbert and Bertrand Gachot were both determined to win this one: Johnny wanted the championship the right way and Bertrand was in his native land. You could expect neither to give way, and neither did. Through the right-hand part of the sweep of Eau Rouge they were neck and neck, rubbing wheels. It looked like Gachot may run out of road but he kept his foot rooted. The momentum carried the pair over to the right and Johnny kept his boot firmly planted, too.'

They collided.

'Bodywork, in the form of Gachot's rear under-deck, shot skywards and the two cars broke away before colliding again. Herbert cannoned hard into the barrier on the right before careering across the circuit in front of the pack and slamming into the opposite armco. Consider that during all of this Martin Donnelly felt the pair had held him up through the section — and that Thomas Danielsson was all but alongside him — and you begin to appreciate how close we came to one of the most monumental shunts of all time. It's bloody quick there. Out of the wrecked car, an ashen-faced Herbert ran back down the hill, where he was going to have to spectate the re-start.'

Johnny was so quick he'd get out in the lead and he'd get bored

---

Herbert was to become champion in a bizarre way. The starting grid was the downhill one no longer used for Formula 1, and when the signal was given to set off on the parade lap Gachot, pole, barely moved. His team manager Glenn Waters explained: 'It's a classic case. If you get the brakes hot, line up facing down a hill and hold the car on the brakes the pads lock on. I told my boys to ram it into gear and keep off the brakes.'

Gachot eventually got going, but at the back of the field, and now faced a desperate decision because, in these circumstances, he ought to have started from the rear of the grid — and he couldn't win from there. As the grid formed, he nosed through to his pole position, but doing that carried a 1-minute penalty. Perhaps he reasoned that losing a minute was more advantageous than starting from the back. Not that it mattered. He was classified 19th.

Jordan himself has a provocative view of the season. 'What was Johnny like in the Formula 3 car? One of the things I often think — I'm not sure if it's 100% true and it may sound preposterous — is that Johnny was so quick he'd get out in the lead and he'd get bored. He wanted to have some fun and he'd slow down to let the rest of them catch him up. That used to drive me mad. To be honest, I'm sure he used to let Gachot catch him up, then they'd be banging wheels and then they couldn't get away from each other.

'It was obvious how much speed he had: he'd either get the big lead or he'd lose a bit of concentration — and therefore lose some speed as well — and *then* catch up without thinking. That's what used to happen. It was all too easy, it was effortless, wasn't it?'

Jane Herbert says the laid-back part of Johnny comes from her side of the family. 'I am like my father. I mean, that aggravated my mother because dad was so laid-back. Dad was lovely really, but it can be frustrating. I remember well that even when John won the Formula 3 championship it didn't dawn on me how important that was, because he was so laid-back about it. I didn't realise it would be the making of him. I was thrilled to bits, but I never thought he could go on from there.'

He could.

The moment. Johnny Herbert wins the 1995 British Grand Prix — the most popular win in the world (Formula One Pictures).

On top of the world at Silverstone, hoisted there by Jean Alesi (left) and David Coulthard (ICN UK Bureau).

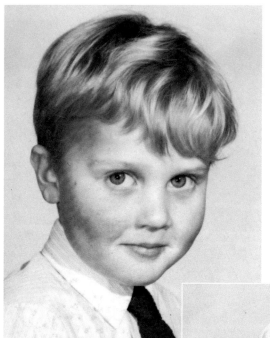

The child is the father of the man — and he did look angelic, didn't he? (Herbert Family).

North Romford Comprehensive — can you spot him? It's not as easy as you think (Herbert family).

Where almost all of them begin, in a kart and smiling (Herbert family).

*Herbert —
number 69 —
exploring
opposite lock?*
(Herbert
family).

*The Junior
World
Championships
in Luxembourg,
1978 — the first
time the
Herberts had
been abroad.
Johnny eyes the
kart* (Herbert
family).

*International
line-up at
Luxembourg*
(Herbert
family).

Push and shove. A meeting in Fano, Italy (Herbert family).

Lakeside snapshot on the Continent, coming back from a meeting (Herbert family).

Mentor and guide. Bill Sisley in his office at Buckmore Park (Bill Sisley).

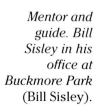

Pensive at Brands Hatch, 1984 (Herbert family).

The Quest 1600 at Brands (Herbert family).

Now, this is how you do it. Nigel Mansell is the instructor (Herbert family).

Throwing the crutches away. Rio testing, 1989 (Formula One Pictures).

The deceptive debut at Rio with Benetton (Formula One Pictures).

The plight of Lotus in 1991 — where are all the sponsors' logos? (Formula One Pictures).

Herbert giving the author an in-depth interview (Sutton Photographic).

The interview (continued). Mika Hakkinen acts as technical consultant (Sutton Photographic).

Above *Beware oncoming traffic. Herbert in the Lotus, Germany, 1992* (Formula One Pictures).

Below *The extraordinary (and largely forgotten) drive to fourth in the wet-dry-wet European Grand Prix at Donington, 1993* (Formula One Pictures).

Right *Early season difficulties, 1995 — a crash in Argentina* (ICN UK Bureau).

The traditional post-race musical knees-up at Silverstone, sweeter because Herbert had won the race. Eddie Jordan with drumsticks, Damon Hill on guitar (Formula One Pictures).

Right With daughter Aimelia, 1995 (Formula One Pictures).

A kiss from wife Becky at Silverstone (Formula One Pictures).

Triumph at Monza, 1995 (ICN UK Bureau).

Brief moments of joy with Sauber in 1996 — Herbert survives the mayhem at Monaco to finish third (ICN UK Bureau).

• CHAPTER THREE •

The battering

EVERYTHING IS DISTORTED because too much happened too fast. At Brands Hatch on 21 August 1988, 17 cars travelled quite normally along the little straight at the back of the pits, twisted left up the incline, crested that and were stretching out into the country. Eleven seconds later three cars were wildly mauled, two others had rammed the barrier with immense ferocity and all but one of the rest was butting and bumping amidst a scrapyard of wreckage.

Johnny Herbert was trapped in what remained of his car, his feet protruding from the front. He was 24. He would never walk properly again, and for long, anxious hours it seemed much worse than that.

I must be careful not to imply that Herbert became famous for his limp, but inevitably it separated him from the others. When he'd recovered he'd make self-mocking descriptions like, 'People always know who I am. I'm the one whose bum sticks out when I walk.' He'd discuss pain, but with a complete absence of self-pity, almost as if he was talking about somebody else.

He'd gone to Brands Hatch, the seventh round of the Formula 3000 Championship, third; no bad place to be in a strong year. Eddie Jordan had partnered him with Danielsson; meanwhile Trevor Foster joined Jordan 'partly because I had such a high regard for Johnny. I was very pleased to come and work with him in 3000 in 1988.'

Formula 3000 close-up, vintage 1988 (Formula One Pictures).

Straight line speed 1988 before disaster came (Formula One Pictures).

It went well from the beginning, Jerez in April. During the winter Herbert had tested the Benetton there, and as a consequence understood the circuit. 'It's a difficult place to set the car up for,' he'd say, 'because the surface is so abrasive that the rear tyres tend to go off very quickly, causing vicious oversteer. It requires a lot of concentration because there are so many corners — nowhere to take a breather — and the only way you can make a lot of time up is under braking and traction out of the corners. In a race, overtaking is almost impossible except at the hairpin, when you can drive down the inside and still find good grip. I suppose a flyer out of the chicane might work, but at most of the corners attempts to pass will ruin your exit speeds and you'll lose out again.'

Foster says, 'We went to Jerez to do the testing, got the car quite late. The whole 3000 deal was put together late. It was Eddie, Adrian Reynard and Alex Hawkridge [once of Toleman in Formula 1] that made it happen. We did the testing and stayed on for the race. Of course the thing was *we don't know how far we'll be able to go in the season, Johnny, but we'll give it our best shot.* Eddie said to him, "It's important for us to get a good result here, Johnny," and he put it on pole.'

Herbert averaged 100 mph and on the hot lap 'I went over the kerbs at the chicane and really *animalled* it.' At the green light Herbert made a clean start, the car shivering a little as the power came on. 'I really went for it in the first two laps and I was a bit surprised that nobody came with me. That made my job a lot easier and I was able to pace myself earlier. Mark Blundell put in fast laps from time to time, but I was watching the boards and I didn't think he could keep it up.' He had only one moment of alarm when, lapping Andy Wallace at the hairpin, he made his move late with Wallace already committed to turning in. They j-u-s-t missed.

'Johnny won the race. Brilliant,' Foster says. 'I mean, he drove brilliantly because it was very hot and he'd never done a race distance as such in the 3000 car. He'd only ever done 20 laps at a time, and here we were going in to something three times as long as that. So he had the heat, the distance, a new car — the first Reynard 3000 car — and he won.'

At Vallelunga he qualified on the second row, but after 45 laps tried to take Gregor Foitek for second place. Out of the spoon-shaped corner at the back of the pits Foitek seemed to have left a gap, his Lola wobbled and Herbert clouted it. The impact sent Herbert off at an angle and the car hit the armco sideways. *Autosport* reported that 'the savage impact tore through the sidepod, bursting a radiator, and Johnny's helmet took a heavy knock, probably from the cockpit surround. He sat stunned and was helped out suffering whiplash and bruising.'

'Qualifying,' Foster says, 'was a bit disappointing because we'd tested there earlier and been quick. Subsequently we found that we were getting into an engine mapping problem, which meant the engine was quite down on power. [Engine mapping is when you plug in a computer which 'reads' what the engine is doing.] As usual, Johnny tried to compensate for that [by pushing hard] and did an absolutely outstanding job. In the race he was running third all over the back of Foitek — he was trying to find a way by. Foitek made a mistake at the hairpin, Johnny went up the inside, Foitek came back off the kerb and straight into the side of Johnny.

'The car hit the armco very badly and Johnny was slightly concussed. He was unconscious when they took him out of the car, and when they released him from the Medical Centre some time later it was obvious he was not OK. He said he felt OK, but he was a bit dazed and he was rambling when he was talking.

'When we got him back to England, Eddie, Peter Collins [Benetton had an option on Herbert until the end of September] and Alex decided that they'd get Professor Watkins [the resident Formula 1 doctor] to have a look at him. The Prof did have a look, carried out some tests and said, "He's not quite right, there's something not mended yet." We did a test at Silverstone and basically it wasn't the Johnny Herbert we knew — he wasn't handling the car as cleanly as he should have been, he wasn't turning in at the same point every time. To be honest, he was struggling with it, although he said — like all racing drivers always say — *I'm fine*. A decision was made not to let him take part in the next race, at Pau, which I still stand by. I think Johnny, however, still regrets it; but Pau was such a dangerous place, and if you didn't feel at ease with it, or if you went there with head damage — if you want to call it that — and had another accident . . .'

Herbert had been complaining of headaches, and Watkins recommended ten days' rest, which brought him back for round 4 at

Silverstone. He qualified in mid-grid and ran fifth but finished seventh, the engine 'hiccoughing'. As Foster says, 'We still hadn't solved this engine mapping problem. In one way it wasn't enough that you could notice, but in another Johnny was having to drive a blinder to get us there, so that's why we felt we had a poor result at Silverstone.'

He was aggressive and he was racing and he was overtaking and they loved it

At Monza he qualified towards the front of the grid and ran eighth. Into the second chicane he nipped out and took a Dutchman, Cor Euser, and set off after Blundell whose engine was misbehaving. A crash stopped the race and at the re-start Herbert charged. *Autosport* reported that 'his car control was a joy to behold. Time and time again the yellow car arrived at the first chicane its braking left to the last moment, millimetre perfect. Then it was over the kerb, stab, stab, stab on the power and he was away, up the gearbox, deft flicks of opposite lock balancing the tail all the while. The crowd loved it, going wild every time he appeared. "It was magic," recalled Herbert later. "They were right behind me, waving me on. I was loving every second, apart from the fact I wasn't leading . . ."'

He finished third.

'At Monza,' Foster says, 'Johnny absolutely drove out of his skin. We had a problem. The starter failed on the grid [at the re-start]. Instead of allowing us to push-start the car [for the parade lap] the marshals made us take it off the grid. We'd gone to pull it back for the push-start and they said *no, no, you must begin from the pit lane*. We did that, unjammed the starter, fired her up and off he went — rose from last, set the lap record, which stood for something like three years, was awesome and finished third. The journalists were coming up afterwards muttering *fantastic watching him through the chicanes*. The crowd was Italian, of course, and Italians particularly delight in anybody who's driving like that. He was aggressive and he was racing and he was overtaking and they loved it. There's no doubt he would have gone all the way to a victory had the race been long enough. He simply ran out of laps.'

At Enna he qualified on the second row. 'By this time, believe it or not, we still hadn't got to the bottom of the engine problem,' Foster says. 'Enna is basically a power circuit. The carbon clutch blew up because for some reason Johnny decided to do one or two practice starts on the warm-up lap and the clutch gave out. By the time he got round on to the grid it had gone. We'd practised with the carbon clutch before but not raced it.' That was 17 July and Brands Hatch was next.

The week before Brands, Herbert tested a Lotus at Monza: Benetton only had an option, remember. He had been invited by Peter Warr, then running Lotus, and at one point was faster than the team's leading driver, thrice World Champion Nelson Piquet. During the test, evidently, Herbert rode the kerbing and was briefly airborne.

Years later I was interviewing Warr for a book on the Britons who have won the Championship (*Champions*, MRP). I explained that for the chapter on Jim Clark, and specifically when Clark entered the RAC Rally, I'd spoken to his navigator and the navigator recounted how they'd plunged off the road in darkness and barrel-rolled across a field. When they finally came to a halt Clark explained that *while* they were barrel-rolling he was trying to work out how he had made the mistake and simultaneously keep his foot off the accelerator in order not to blow the engine.

Warr understood (he had worked with Clark at Lotus) and cited the example of Herbert at Monza who, after being airborne, returned to the pits and clinically dissected what had happened. Warr realised that Herbert — despite the possible importance of the test, despite the alarming possibilities of being airborne — continued to think calmly and logically while *he* was in the air.

We concluded that the really good drivers have different reaction processes from ordinary people. And mentioning all this to Mike Thompson moved him to say, 'Yes, that's how he is, he's fatalistic and even in the air it wouldn't occur to him to worry about it.'

Brands was a strange, sombre, strained weekend, not least because in the Saturday free practice Frenchman Michel Trolle crashed at high speed and was seriously injured. Herbert, now partnered by Donnelly — Danielsson had eye trouble — took pole, Donnelly alongside. Herbert got down to 1:14.77, Donnelly 1:15.00, Foitek 1:15.54, Pierluigi Martini 1:15.63. *Autosport* reported that 'Herbert

The crucial Rio test before the 1989 season (Formula One Pictures).

sat out most of the final session, watching the monitors, eyeing the fruitless on-track struggle before popping out and dropping in a nonchalant 1:15.58 just to remind them who was boss.'

'Before Brands,' Foster says, 'we finally did get to the bottom of this engine mapping problem, and we'd also tried a couple of small new tweaks on the car. We went to Donington testing and Johnny flew round. I think the engine was performing for the first time as it should have been.

'At Brands Johnny was just so confident. The regulations allowed you three sets of tyres for the weekend. He went out in the first session, he was miles quicker than anybody else on something like his second lap, and at the end of the session he had provisional pole by three-quarters of a second.

'The second session was amazing. It gave me a feeling I don't think I've ever had before: he was so much quicker than everybody else, and you kept thinking *this can't be right, this has to be wrong* because you were waiting for all the others to catch up and they never did. He went out, did a run which equalled the time he'd done in the first session, then just sat there with new tyres on. We were only going to use them if anybody got near us and nobody did — so we only used one set of tyres for qualifying!'

On race day — the Sunday — visitors to Herbert's pit included Collins, Ken Tyrrell and Frank Williams, who was widely rumoured to have a contract in his pocket for Herbert. Eddie Jordan says that 'as far as I can recall, Frank Williams brought his motorhome round to the back of the pits [presumably so he could meet people in private]. Tyrrell was there because he was presenting the prizes. Did Frank have a contract to sign Johnny? I had been speaking to him for some time and I've a good idea the way Frank works. He is also very pro British drivers. I think he would have been interested in having a closer look at what Johnny was doing — I think he had a view to looking to sign him.'

The biggest motor racing crash of the 1980s had begun

Ian Blackman was there, spectating. Bill Sisley sat in the grandstand opposite the pits, spectating. Bob and Jane Herbert were in a hospitality unit opposite the pits, spectating. So was Mike Thompson, although a different hospitality suite. He was with a couple of sponsors, all three spectating. Foster busied himself in the pits.

It had drizzled in the morning, but that had gone. From pole Herbert made a lovely start, power and adhesion perfectly balanced to lead from Donnelly. 'They set off,' Foster says, 'and when they came into sight at Clearways on the first lap there was Johnny and Martin and then a b-i-g gap before the rest came through. Martin held on to Johnny for the first four or five laps, then decided *if I keep this pace up I'm going to crash* and let Johnny go. Johnny pulled away — he was on autopilot, long gone.'

A crash on lap 24 between Roberto Moreno and Foitek stopped it. The story of Johnny Herbert's life would have been quite different if it hadn't, and there is greater irony than even that.

Foster explains it. 'When they stopped the race, Johnny was six or seven seconds in front of Martin, and Martin was 11 seconds or whatever in front of the third-placed man. Then Moreno had an accident.

The annoying part about it is that his car wasn't in a dangerous place. They could have moved it under yellow [caution] flags, but they panicked and stopped the race.'

Bob Herbert echoes that. 'The crash happened right underneath us. The car wasn't in a dangerous place — Moreno's car wasn't dangerous. If Moreno had got hold of Foitek he'd have killed him. Moreno was absolutely livid.'

Another view is that Moreno's car was in the 'launch position', meaning that if another car struck it that other car might have been launched and, however likely or unlikely such a scenario might be, you play safe, halt proceedings and clear it all away.

A few drops of rain had fallen.

'Johnny sat there waiting for the re-start very calm and relaxed,' Foster says. At the green he got too much wheelspin and was third into Paddock, Donnelly and Martini ahead, Foitek behind. Herbert and Foitek had rubbed wheels accelerating from the grid and maybe that set a tone, maybe not. The geography of Brands allowed pit crews to watch the start then nip through the pit and watch as the cars descended from Druids. Foster did that. From the hospitality suite, Bob and Jane would also be able to see the cars come down from Druids, but then be obscured by the transporters in the paddock.

Foster watched as they came 'down from Druids through Bottom Bend and went out on to the Grand Prix circuit' — the left twist up the incline. 'Johnny went down the outside, Foitek went to the inside to protect the inside line, and Johnny was going to try and get the better exit. I could see this happening up the hill, but then they went out of sight. I think on the crest of the hill Foitek started to move across but you couldn't really see Johnny.'

The biggest motor racing crash of the 1980s had begun.

They were moving on to the fastest part of the circuit: a long dip, which, as it rose towards Hawthorn corner, was known as Hawthorn Hill. Two years before, the mid-point of the dip had been the second Longines timing point for the British Grand Prix and recorded Formula 1 cars at 201 mph. The Formula 3000 cars wouldn't reach that, but they were already accelerating up towards 150 mph.

Herbert and Foitek touched.

That turned Herbert's car to an angle across Foitek's front right wheel. The cars veered off the track together, crossing the narrow

Left *Happy to be in Grand Prix racing at last* (Formula One Pictures).

strip of grass and battering again the base of a bridge spanning the track. The impact flung them backwards, still together but pieces being wrenched from the cars, directly into the path of Olivier Grouillard. He was helpless. He struck them so violently that he burst *through* them, pitching Herbert over the narrow grass strip on the right and into the barrier; punting Foitek away to the left. This impact twisted Grouillard and, at an angle now, he rammed the barrier about 20 metres further on than Herbert.

What remained of Herbert's car rotated once on the grass and the centrifugal force kept it rotating four more times until it was back on the track. Its thrashing ceased and it came to rest facing the oncoming traffic.

What remained of Grouillard's car spun six times and came to rest across the track.

What remained of Foitek's car contorted sideways on the grass strip, pirouetted so that for an instant it leant over the barrier, brushed the top of the barrier, landed, rolled and came to rest on the grass shrouded in smoke.

Blundell, running behind Grouillard, saw Olivier ram Herbert and Foitek. He instinctively swerved left-left-left away, somehow threaded through. Behind him, like a shoal of frightened fish, cars darted in all directions. One veered through the flying debris and butted the barrier. Another spun towards the barrier at Herbert's side, helplessly clipped Herbert, then hit the barrier. Another slithered and struck the barrier on the left. With amazing reaction and bravery — the last car had only just stopped — two marshals sprinted across the track towards Herbert.

Sue Page, in charge of the St John's Ambulance team, was seven months pregnant, so 'I wasn't working-working. If you're properly on duty, in an emergency you're expected to do your share of the lifting and carrying — not a good idea when you are very, very pregnant. So what I was doing was overseeing.'

She sat in the medical car at the Medical Centre, which is to the side of the incline and therefore very close to the accident.

'The medical car was called out — I suppose by the Clerk of the Course — because it always goes first and straight away. I stayed in it, so I was one of the first on the scene. It was so chaotic that I put out a message *would every ambulance make its way to Hawthorns slowly.'*

This is not as contrary as it sounds. The rescue vehicles — with doctors, stretchers and cutting equipment — are scrambled at once, and what you don't need, as they do their work, are ambulances charging into their midst.

Neil Harper, an ambulanceman on duty at Paddock, heard the call over the radio: 'I'd never heard that before — all ambulances to one incident. From Paddock we drove the ambulance round the track but we didn't go mad. It took, I suppose, about a minute. You couldn't see anything going up the incline, but over it you saw total devastation. The ambulances parked up in a line.'

Come on Johnny, calm down.
Come on Johnny, breathe, breathe

'Because of the condition I was in,' Sue Page says, 'and because I wasn't working-working, I took it on myself that I would stay back and park all the ambulances in a row. There were five. The attendants from each would go down and get a casualty each, meaning that they were to take care of a driver stuck in a car, then, as and when everything was ready, we'd send the ambulance down.'

'The race was red flagged straight away,' Foster says, 'and Johnny didn't come round. Chris Witty [formerly of Toleman] was with us at the time because he was sponsorship co-ordinator for Q8 [a Jordan sponsor]. We ran up to the control tower and asked, 'What's happened? What's happened?' There was a lot of confusion, nobody knew. They said Johnny's had a big accident. The doctor was going out so we jumped in his car and out we went.'

Bob Herbert thinks only one car came round, which had to mean something enormous must have stopped all the others 'You're always a little bit fearful. We ran to the tunnel under the track, then ran on to the pits and nobody really knew what was going on.'

Sisley, in the grandstand, 'saw Johnny had a problem at the re-start. I saw them go up the hill, then nothing, then an announcement over the tannoy. It had gone quiet and I thought *this is big.* You do think that, you know, when it goes quiet. I tried to put it out of my mind because when you have personal feelings towards somebody who might be involved — well, I just blank it out.'

Thompson remembers that 'Donnelly got a bit of a flyer at the re-start and I always think that if Johnny had got off the line well it all wouldn't have happened. He wouldn't have been engulfed by the bloody field. We saw them going up the hill then we heard about it over the tannoy.'

Foster remembers that 'when we got there Johnny was in the car and obviously very much in shock. He was sitting there shouting *put me out, put me out, put me out*. He was in a massive amount of pain. Immediately you could see his legs out of the front of the car. You looked and thought *they are not the shape they should be*. I don't think he'd been hurt in the first impact, but when the car came back across the circuit with the frontal chassis missing into the armco the opposite side, that's when all the damage was done to his feet. Eventually they were trying to put the oxygen mask on him. *Come on Johnny, calm down. Come on Johnny, breathe, breathe.*'

In fact it wasn't oxygen but Entonex, a pain-killing gas that works immediately — injections can take 20 minutes and would be administered later. Entonex comes from a portable cylinder and reaches the mask through a tube with a valve. Some casualties are reluctant to inhale it — maybe fearing they'll choke — but once they do start, and their bodies feel the benefit, they tend to inhale more and more deeply and with gathering urgency. It can cause a chemical reaction within the gas, making it freeze in the tube. This is what Herbert did, and the two medics treating him kept putting their hands on to the valve to warm it.

The man who organised the paddock and sorted out any problems there, Danny Miller, was in touch with Race Control by radio and went to the scene in a car. 'I saw carnage. I saw the armco damaged before the bridge where Johnny had hit it, and I saw the impact of where Johnny had ended up on the other side of the bridge. I had to assess the number of cars involved and report back to Race Control. I think you'll find there were 11. Johnny was in the cockpit and emergency equipment was being brought from the rescue vehicles and ambulances. I could see his feet sticking out and they were in a very bad state.' Miller remembers that Herbert had been given the pain killer 'to relieve him while they extricated him from the car'.

Left *Portrait of relaxation, with Benetton, 1989* (Formula One Pictures).

Jane Herbert remembers that 'somebody must have said John was involved. Bertrand Gachot came up and said *don't worry, he's OK.*'

Bob Herbert remembers that 'Frank Williams was down there. Did he say something or was it someone who was with him? We went across to the Medical Centre thinking John would be taken there. Either people didn't want to tell you the extent of what had happened or they didn't know.' Jane remembers going into the Medical Centre 'and they were very nice to us'. Bob agrees, but 'they didn't take him to the Medical Centre, did they?'

Actually, they did and they didn't. 'Once I'd got the ambulances all sorted,' Sue Page says, 'I came back to the Medical Centre and sat with his parents. He was in quite a bad way and what happens is that drivers aren't just taken to hospital, they are brought to the Medical Centre first to stabilise their condition, because a journey can be horrendous.'

At the scene, Foster watched as the medical team 'stabilised him and made sure everything was OK before they moved him. They got him out of the car' — it was now 40 minutes after the crash — 'and put him in the ambulance.'

To stabilise him before he was taken to St Mary's Hospital, Sidcup, the ambulance backed up to the rear of the Medical Centre where a nurse, Marion Day, waited. Herbert remained in the ambulance while they were 'running drips out and fluids because when you have breaks like that you lose an awful lot of blood.' She 'dressed his feet. They were (pause) . . . messy. You could see the ankle bones. I thought *you will never walk again.*'

Foster says that 'Witty and I went back to the pits and said *big shunt, it's his ankles.* Years before, Johnny Cecotto had had a bad crash at Brands driving a Toleman, sustaining severe leg injuries, and Witty was there then. He said we'd better go to the hospital because one of Herbert's feet is quite bad and we must make sure they don't decide to amputate it. That would have been the end of the career.'

The ambulance left Brands for Sidcup. Neil Harper was charged with tending Herbert during the journey. 'His overalls were all cut [for the drips] because no way could you take them off. He had a tee-shirt underneath. My job was to hold his arms. He'd got the drips in them and you must be careful because they can get ripped off — he was drugged, he was the equivalent of being drunk. He asked *how many times have I been World Champion?* I didn't take any notice at first. He kept asking so I said *once*. He made that noise of triumph — *yaahoo* — and waved his arms. All the way to hospital that's what he was asking. I held his arms and I kept varying the numbers. I'd tell him he'd been World Champion once, then three times or maybe four times just to keep him happy. When we reached the hospital we took him in and a nurse came up and cut his tee-shirt away. He said *not my tee-shirt!* and she looked at him as it if was a strange thing to say, and he smiled.'

Foster says that 'we got straight in a car, went to the hospital, saw the doctor there and said *it's Johnny Herbert, a racing driver. Whatever you do, please make sure you keep the foot on* — it was only hanging by a bit of skin. The reply was *we'll do our best.*'

Mike Thompson 'went off in a car following the ambulance to hospital.' Blackman had been 'just spectating. I used to go to all Johnny's races and I'd been standing on the outside at Paddock. I went with Mike straight to the hospital and we waited there to make sure it was going to be all right because everybody was a bit doom and gloom — everybody thought *that's it, he won't drive again, probably won't even walk again.*'

Jane says that eventually she and Bob 'must have realised they were going to take him straight to hospital. I can't think who took us.' In fact, Sue Page organised a lift for them because 'we never feel that people in the sort of state they would be in should drive themselves.'

Bob explains that 'the whole thing is a bit of a blur', and Jane repeats that exactly: 'A bit of a blur.' Bob remembers reaching the hospital and 'standing around. Becky was there by then. Mike Thompson and Ian Blackman and Trevor Foster were all sitting around and nobody really knew, it was a total blank. A doctor brought out something and I signed it, didn't even know what I was signing. They might have had to amputate his left foot and it was probably a disclaimer. I signed that and really I didn't know what it was . . .'

Jane ruminates that in those circumstances 'you don't know, do you?'

Bob remembers that 'we were just walking round and round in a daze.'

Sue Page remembers 'some of the drivers came to the Medical Centre and said they'd run over Johnny's feet — because his boots were in the middle of the track. His boots had actually come off his feet with the laces done up.'

Neil Harper remembers the drive back to Brands with a doctor and a paramedic, 'and we said *that's the end of his career* because we'd seen the state of his feet and there was no way that we could see that they could be repaired.'

We still weren't sure whether he would ever drive again

Foster remembers the waiting at St Mary's. 'His parents were there. I don't know what time it was but very late at night — several hours later — the surgeon who did the operation said *obviously it's a bit of a mess but we've put everything back together as best we can*. I still maintain that if it had been you or I hurt in a normal road accident, they'd probably have taken the foot off. The surgeon said *but I'm afraid his sporting days are over.*'

Bob remembers that 'we saw him first when he was in intensive care. Trolle was in there as well. John was hallucinating, he was really bad.'

Jane found it 'dreadful to see. Dreadful. I mean, I smile about it now because when he was in intensive care the idea was just to talk to him as he lay there. I said to him *see over there, that's Michel Trolle* and John whistled. I'll never forget it. He kept whistling to Trolle to try and attract his attention — but John wasn't with it, you know what I mean? Whistling! I couldn't believe it.'

Bob is sure his son was 'in agony'.

Foster says that 'about half an hour after the surgeon came out we went in to see Johnny. He had both legs in huge plaster casts. We had a brief chat although he couldn't tell who we were.'

Thompson remembers that 'at St Mary's they had the guy that got the really badly broken leg from the day before [Trolle]. They showed us his X-rays and his leg was about 12 inches long. Johnny had been operated on and he was drugged. I remember saying *you'll be back in six weeks*, which he wasn't, but he wasn't far from it, either. The surgeon told us — and he was 100% correct — that the most serious thing broken was a certain bone, and if you don't get any blood to it the ankle fuses. That's what happened and that's Johnny's legacy of the crash. One ankle fused. The father of the guy who caused it [Foitek] came to the hospital saying *it's not my son's fault, it's not my son's fault.*'

McCarthy was at Oulton Park racing and 'suddenly a couple of people approached me with sombre faces. *What's wrong?* They said *it's Johnny.* I asked what had happened, but they only said *it's touch and go.* I immediately got in my car and drove at about 140 miles an hour and I was at the hospital very, very quickly. I walked straight in. Bob and Jane and Becky were all there and they told me about the crash and his feet and ankles. Instantly I felt a sense of relief because that was survivable, but then I was concerned about what it was going to do to his career if they were that bad.'

Blackman remembers that 'we visited John again later and we still weren't sure whether he would ever drive again.' To which McCarthy adds, 'I went to the hospital every day — or every other day — to see him to try and keep his spirits up. He was in a state, his feet were in a bad state. The surgeons were showing me the X-rays and what used to be bone structure now looked like a map of the Caribbean.

'When Johnny got home he was still obviously going through an awful lot of pain, but he was quiet and introverted. He'd just rub his legs and you knew the pain was there but he didn't go on about it. He's not one to do that. He was very, very brave all the way through, and resilient.'

Bob Herbert confesses that 'I had never really worried about racing before. I had never even thought you'd have an accident or anything like that. It brought it home. Now I watch the racing heart in mouth. I have done ever since then.'

Six weeks after the accident, the racing school at Brands Hatch was holding a final test day for young hopefuls and invited Herbert to make the presentations. He turned up with crutches and recognised Danny Miller, 'even though he'd been drugged up to the eye-balls, recognised my face from the scene and, via me, sent his thanks to all the rescue services, which I thought was very nice.'

Trying to rescue the career, Herbert drives for Tyrrell in Belgium, 1989
(Formula One Pictures).

Herbert was working hard to regain full fitness and one of the incentives was provided by Collins and Benetton, because Herbert was due to have a test with them in December, something that might lead to a full contract. 'Benetton lent us a monocoque, we fitted it up with pedals and he could exercise in it,' Thompson says. 'The pedals were set at their proper pressure. I remember him exercising and breaking down and crying at one point because it was so painful. He didn't shirk exercise — well, he did [in general] because he was a lazy bastard! — but he didn't shirk anything because of pain.

'I come back to the fatalism. I was constantly asking him *is it going to be all right John, is it going to be all right? What do you think?* He'd say *I dunno,* and he didn't know. To a certain extent that has always worked against him because in motor racing you have to be positive in what you do. He was fatalistic in the sense of *it will either come good or it won't come good and that's it, I'm completely neutral between those two situations. I'll do my best and see what happens.*'

I want to expand on this, using examples, because it is both relevant and important to a true understanding of Herbert.

He told me a little while after Brands Hatch, when I asked if the accident had changed him: 'No, it hasn't. I mean, I'm the same as I was before. Why give up? It's happened. It doesn't trouble me at all. It's done, I've smashed them up, now I've got to get on with the rest of my life.'

To supplement those words, I reproduce a section of dialogue from my interview with Bob and Jane Herbert in the summer of 1996.

Bob: 'I have never seen a hard side to John. He keeps a lot of emotions within himself, which isn't always good.'

Jane: 'That goes right back to when he was young. He never could show his emotions, could he, Bob?'

Bob: 'No.'

Jane: 'He gets very frustrated inside, very frustrated. He's very deep. He has been right from his schooling. This is where the problems have been, I think.'

Bob: 'I wouldn't have thought there was a real hard side to him. And if I point things out to him, he'll say *what are you worrying about? Don't worry about it.*'

Jane: 'But he is worried about it.'

Bob: 'In the aftermath of Brands I never saw him cry. When he was laying in hospital and we were worried about his career — because that's all he'd done to earn his living — he wasn't worried. *If they cut my foot off, I've got a stump, haven't I? I only need my left foot for the clutch . . .'*

This makes Jane hoot with laughter because, frankly, for your son to talk in this way is wonderfully mad.

Bob: '*If they cut this knee off* — well, John wasn't worried because *they can fix something on there and I can still drive.* As long as he could still drive, that's all he was interested in.'

Jane: 'Remember that stump he talked about?'

Bob: 'Yes. *I don't need my foot, do I? What do I want my foot for?'*

So Herbert embarked on a long struggle to be physically capable of driving again. Blackman says that 'Mike Thompson did a lot for him, sent him to different clinics and had all the right bits done for him.'

Out of the car he's still pretty fragile, he's still using his crutches

---

Thompson himself says that 'as soon as Johnny came out of hospital he went off to Austria because Peter Collins was keen for him to go to an Austrian specialist for rehabilitation. The doctor here said, "Whatever you do, tell them not to take your leg out of the plaster because we've got to get blood to that bone." Johnny flew to Austria and that night phoned me up. *I'm in a swimming pool and they've taken the plaster off already!* Their views were completely different.'

Thompson obtained two karts, altered one so Herbert could fit in and stuck lead weights to his helmet to build up the neck muscles. Thompson then brought Herbert to Buckmore Park and Bill Sisley again. 'He came in a wheelchair,' Sisley says, 'and they had to lift him out of the wheelchair into the kart. He drove it with minimal leg movement.'

Thompson explains that 'because he was going to have the Benetton test we got a couple of karts and took them to Buckmore, which is just up the road. I drove round with him so he could get used to something close, and also it would make it a little less boring. We tried a motocross boot on his dodgy leg to protect it. We wrapped the leg in foam. First time out I felt really sorry for him because he was quite slow, but at the end of the day he was right on it. We went two or three times a week for about a month, pounding round and round and round.' Blackman remembers that they'd go as many days as they could, trying to get him back into it again.

In mid-December Herbert did test the Benetton at Silverstone. 'Freezing cold day and he was bloody quick,' Thompson says. 'The first couple of laps the car was driving him, then the third or fourth lap he was away.' He covered 30 laps.

Collins said at the time, 'He did all we wanted him to do first time out. For a first run in a car since his accident at Brands Hatch it was an encouraging performance.'

Benetton signed Herbert to partner Sandro Nannini.

Reviewing the decision, Collins told me then: 'We have one experienced driver in Nannini who has to accept more responsibility and develop, and one newcomer in Herbert, who may develop more quickly — or slowly — than we expect. Herbert? You watch drivers, you follow their careers when they're young, and when you've been in this business long enough you know what makes a good driver tick. You look for things when he's out on the circuit — style, smoothness, general control of the situation, winning ability.

'We took an interest in Johnny after he'd done an exceptional job in the Festival at Brands, come from behind and won it by a very long way. And in a Formula 3 race I remember he looked very slow and yet there were only two people who were quicker. Stewart, Lauda, Prost, they never looked quick!

'Herbert is the most likeable bloke you'll meet. What impressed me is that he is so uncomplicated. In an era when drivers are sharp businessmen, he just drives cars well and that's what he does. He had the terrible accident at Brands last season but he has recovered from that very well. We took a monocoque from last year's car, fitted it with seat, pedals, gear-change, and spring-loaded it like the real thing so he could practice in it. And that was when he still had plaster on his left leg! He's done three tests now in the race car. At Silverstone on

Right *Herbert drove the last two Grands Prix of 1990 with Lotus. The engine failed in Japan* (Formula One Pictures).

the first day it was just too wet and the car was aquaplaning, but on the second day he did 265 miles and a 30-lap run with a full fuel load at the end. Out of the car he's still pretty fragile, he's still using his crutches.'

Herbert tested the Benetton at Silverstone again in January, tested at Paul Ricard in the south of France — where, reportedly, he found his first serious test session heavy going on his legs — tested at Rio. *Autosport* reported that 'despite countless rumours that all is not well with Johnny Herbert's legs, the Benetton team is still confident that he will be fully race fit by the start of the season. The officials at the Rio testing were somewhat wary of allowing the young Briton to drive, but once he had proved he could get out of the cockpit in 7 seconds they withdrew any restriction and Herbert went on to complete 650 miles of running. At one point he ran over a bump and banged his legs against the steering column which caused him some pain. "The bump would have hurt anyone," explained team manager Peter Collins, "and it caused him a bit more pain because he had previously injured the leg, but he is in fine shape. If anything, his arms were tiring towards the end of the test, but he'll be on the pace."'

The first race of 1989 was the Brazilian Grand Prix on 26 March. 'I'm still getting grass and grit from Brands Hatch seeping out of the wounds!' he said (typically) as he prepared to make his debut, 'but I threw away my crutches last week and now I am improving in leaps and bounds. I have got completely out of the car in 6.2 seconds so I don't expect any problems.'

Meanwhile a Benetton spokesman revealed that 'there are a lot of jealous drivers, particularly in Italy, who are wondering why Johnny is in the car and they are not. Johnny has withstood this pressure and so has the team.' Hmmm. Beware votes of confidence in motor sport as much as in football.

In the Friday morning free practice he was 11th, and in first qualifying eighth, slipping back to ninth a day later — the fifth row of the grid. He completed the first Grand Prix lap of his career in 1:45.968, eighth. On lap 4 Boutsen (Williams) retired with an engine problem, lifting Herbert to seventh. He ran there to his pit stop on lap 12 for tyres. By lap 17 he was sixth; fifth as Derek Warwick (Arrows) pitted, fourth as Mauricio Gugelmin (March) pitted, third as Riccardo

Patrese (Williams) pitted. That was lap 25 of the 61. Warwick re-took him, Herbert losing grip before his second stop. He sank to sixth, but amidst the second round of pit stops was up to fourth: almost instantly fifth as Patrese went by; fourth again as Patrese's engine failed. He remained there to the end.

No driver had scored points in his first Grand Prix since Alain Prost in Argentina in 1980, and no driver before that since George Follmer (USA) in South Africa in 1973.

Herbert, looking young but not as exhausted as you might have anticipated, said in a voice bearing more London influence than it would subsequently: 'Yeah, it's been good for me. Everybody has been doubting, I think, after the accident I had last year that I wouldn't be fit enough. You know, Benetton stuck with me through everything and we've come through it and we've proved a point — so it's thanks to Benetton and Peter Collins.'

It takes a hell of a long time to get the damn muscles back

The central aspect of Rio was terribly misleading, as Herbert would discover and concede. He had not recovered to anything like the extent he imagined. If he thought he'd just come off the rack, he'd go back on it.

At his second Grand Prix, San Marino at Imola, he qualified on the second last row and finished 11th, two laps down. At his third, Monaco at Monte Carlo, he qualified on the second last row again and finished 14th, four laps down. He rationalised it to me like this: 'Rio was too easy and I know why, because you don't brake so much — and the heat wasn't the problem it might have been. Then I went to Imola with the wrong attitude. I thought *this is easy, I'm going to do it again*. I didn't accept it was my feet until I got to Monaco.'

In sum, his foot lacked the strength to depress a Formula 1 brake pedal.

'They've worked it out that it's about 700 or 800 lbs pressure. I can probably get 250 or 300 with the ball of the foot. It's made smooth movement difficult. I get one corner right but not the next three. It's all luck. Instead of throttle-brake I'm going throttle-feel-for-the-

right-place-brake. I need more strength to push the pedals harder.'
Herbert devised a system where 'rather than put the ball of my foot to
the pedal, I put the pedal half way up the foot — but there's no feel
whatsoever there and it's difficult to gauge.

'I have to do physiotherapy every day and the walking is better. I
can go out shopping and walk nearly all day long.' He also told me
that he wore a 'cooling cap', which had the effect of your brain
telling you that you were freezing when you were sweating. Quite
why anyone should want or need to do this I can't imagine, and I
think that at the time I assumed Herbert had invented it to see if I'd
fall for it and put it into print. 'The crash was purely the ankles and
feet. The left one was near enough ripped off, the right one was
smashed and deformed. It looked like a monkey's foot, not a human
foot. The problem is muscle wastage if you're in hospital for two and
a half months. At Rio, the first time I'd got rid of the walking-sticks,
I didn't have calf muscles. There wasn't anything there at all. It takes
a hell of a long time to get the damn muscles back. Now it's still small
but it looks like a muscle. I spend two and a half hours on the tram-
poline. I stand on my toes for five minutes, bounce on one foot then
the other, lean on to the toes, jump up and down, then I do my bike
riding . . .'

In Mexico he qualified 18th and finished 15th, three laps down; in
the US Grand Prix at Phoenix he qualified on the last row and
slogged a fifth place a lap down despite losing fourth gear late on and
suffering a bit from the right foot. That was 4 June.

At the Canadian Grand Prix it went seriously wrong. In the Friday
morning untimed session he was 26th of 30; 28th in first qualifying,
25th in the Saturday morning untimed session, and 22nd in second
qualifying — but a clutch of drivers who'd been below him improved.
Overall it left him 29th, three places from the race. He found diffi-
culty in disguising his disappointment.

Four days before the French Grand Prix, Benetton issued a state-
ment from Milan. I quote it at length.

'Following discussions between Benetton Formula, Johnny Herbert
and the medical advisors, it has been agreed that Johnny Herbert will
cease driving in World Championship Formula 1 Grands Prix for the
next three months.

On the streets of Adelaide . . .

. . . but the clutch failed (Both Formula One Pictures).

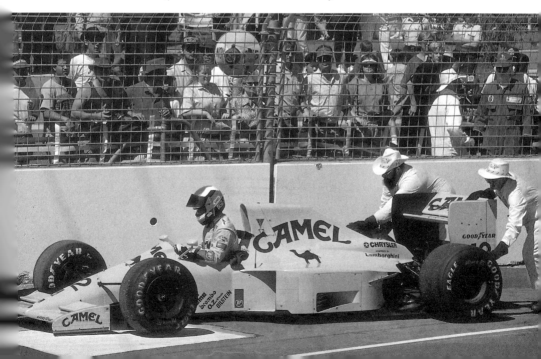

His replacement in the Benetton Ford Team for the French Grand Prix on Sunday July 9 is to be the Italian driver Emanuele Pirro. However, Herbert is to remain under contract to Benetton Formula and will play a major role as a driver in the development of the Benetton Ford B189 and a computerised active suspension system which has been designed by Benetton Formula.

"During the past two months, the brief intervals between each Grand Prix have not allowed me to devote adequate time to the exercise programmes which are so necessary to ensure my full recovery," said Johnny Herbert.

"Although I have not been in pain during Grands Prix, the muscles in my right leg do not yet have sufficient strength for me to drive to the full extent of my ability. In the interest of my long-term future and ultimate recovery I believe that this temporary withdrawal will give me adequate opportunity to work on my legs, free from the pressures created by competition in Formula 1. Everyone in the Benetton Ford Team has been very supportive and I will continue with the testing and development of our new car."

"We have no intention of releasing Johnny Herbert from his contract," said Peter Collins, Team Manager of Benetton Formula. "On the one occasion when Johnny was not limited by the lack of strength in his right leg, he more than demonstrated his potential by finishing fourth in the Brazilian Grand Prix which was his first ever Formula 1 race. We are all convinced of his long-term potential. In the meantime, he will play a major role as a driver in our test and development programmes.'"

Later Herbert told me, 'They said as soon as you're fit we'll put you back in, but I knew that was rubbish. They were putting it nicely. Why do I think they took the decision to get rid of me? I don't know. I think it was a bit of Ford and a bit of Benetton as well, saying *why are you doing so badly?* I felt that was totally stupid. It wasn't just me, it was the whole team. I think I was a way out. It wasn't so much *let's get rid of him because he's not doing well*, it was just a way out. I don't know whose decision it was.

'When Peter told me I was expecting it anyway, so it wasn't so bad. It was a big door that had shut, but probably long-term it's better, because if I'd carried on and gone better in the new car, I still wouldn't have improved. The thing is, when you're racing the races are every two weeks. You come home, you've a week in between, but what I need is constant time to do something solid — my physiotherapy work. I just couldn't do it. I'd do the week then be away for three days (plus travel) at the next Grand Prix. You miss three days of the physiotherapy and that's the equivalent, really, of losing a week. You have to do it every day.'

The week that Benetton gave Herbert the bad news, a great deal was going on in the background. Tyrrell fell out with their driver Michele Alboreto — a tobacco sponsorship dispute — and reached for a Formula 3000 driver, Jean Alesi, to replace Alboreto on a strictly limited basis. In the French Grand Prix Alesi finished fourth (emulating Herbert in scoring on debut). The Alboreto affair wasn't settled, and Tyrrell decided to retain Alesi; and Alesi in turn decided he must do the 3000 races, which coincided with the Grands Prix. Alesi was leading the 3000 Championship.

I've got to tell my brain that my foot is working

The Belgian Grand Prix coincided with the Halfords Birmingham Superprix 3000 and Tyrrell reached for Herbert. 'We are very grateful to Benetton for releasing Johnny,' Ken Tyrrell said. In fact, just before the announcement Herbert had tested the Benetton at Pembrey and said, 'All my hard work in physiotherapy has really begun to pay off. At Pembrey I was able to brake properly with the ball of my foot again, and we put in some pretty quick times. I feel strong and confident, and Spa just can't come soon enough.'

He tested the Tyrrell at Monza — the week Collins left Benetton, incidentally — and said, 'The Tyrrell is different, softer. I'm used to a lot stiffer car and by stiff I mean very stiff. I did 55 laps at Monza and although they weren't back-to-back I feel fine.'

He was speaking at the Tyrrell factory just before Spa and, under questioning, discussed his injuries. I want you to imagine that he is grinning like an imp the whole time, and the irreverence of what he said towards the end — you'll see — is purest, unadulterated Herbert.

'I couldn't brake to the best of my ability because I just didn't have the confidence. The brain was used to the foot not working, so I wasn't allowing myself to use the foot properly — subconsciously — in case I couldn't push the pedal hard enough to stop the car. I've got to tell my brain that my foot is working. It's like me limping. I shouldn't limp, really. Yesterday I had a good day — I looked normal. If I walk slowly I look very normal, if I walk quicker the limp comes back. It's all mental. I have shrunk. I don't really know where it's gone but I've shrunk by maybe an inch. I know one heel got hammered, but that doesn't explain losing an inch on the other heel. I used to be taller than my girlfriend . . .'

On a more pragmatic and less provocative level he said, 'Spa should be good for me. It's hard braking at the hairpin, but you're not going that quick there. If I don't do well it won't be totally the end of my career, but if I do well it will do me a lot of good. If I could beat Pirro that would stick one on them, wouldn't it?' He'd partner Jonathan Palmer.

At Spa he spun on the Friday morning, then went better in the afternoon before spinning again. It was typical Spa, moist and misty. Mike Thompson was there and 'for the first session, in the wet, I was standing down by Eau Rouge. Johnny was probably braking 30 yards later than Palmer by his second lap.' Saturday was cool and overcast. He qualified on the eighth row. A wet race, and on lap 4 Herbert spun off, walked doggedly back to the pits so angry that his brain forgot to tell him to limp.

Portugal coincided with the 3000 at Le Mans and Alesi went there, Herbert went to Estoril, but he struggled again. He failed to qualify by 0.017 second. 'It was lack of drive' he said, fashioning a pun. *'Lack of drive in the driver.* There were no changes needed to the car, just a magic potion for me.' What Herbert did not say was that, the night before, he and Thompson had dined, eaten lobster, which must have been off, and, as Thompson confesses, 'I felt really guilty and Johnny felt really sick.'

Alesi completed the season for Tyrrell.

It was time to look around, maybe take what you could get. In October he teamed up with Donnelly for a Japanese sports car race at Fuji driving a Porsche 962 in a team being 'overseen' by Peter Collins. They finished sixth. 'I'd always wanted to have a go in a Group C car. You've really got to have a bit of variety. If you're in

Riding the storm, Adelaide, 1991 (Formula One Pictures).

Formula 1, obviously they won't let you do it, but if, like me, you're not doing anything you might as well have a go.'

Have a go?

Herbert was waiting to hear from Tyrrell about 1990 and had a Benetton contract for testing. Nissan was interested in an effort for the Le Mans 24 Hour sports car race, and in October he visited the factory at Milton Keynes. Meanwhile Collins murmured about Herbert racing a Porsche. Cumulatively, alas, this is a career going wrong and might have gone further wrong. Before Christmas he travelled to Italy to talk to the small Formula 1 team Osella (which, frankly, was not the place to have a go).

'We went to Italy,' Thompson says, 'because Osella were to sign him. They did a medical, tests for strength, everything, and said *that's good, that's fine*. They X-rayed his foot and said, "Can we do the tests again because we can't believe you can move it." Johnny was incredibly determined.'

111

He didn't get the drive (a good career move).

In January Thompson confirmed that Herbert had been talking to another small Italian Formula 1 team, Coloni, but they'd have to pre-qualify for the Grands Prix and might not, and Herbert needed 'plenty of driving' — so no Coloni (another good career move).

Once the search for drives had resolved itself, Herbert had a test-ing contract with Lotus, nine Japanese Formula 3000 races and six sports car events plus Le Mans in the Porsche. It was what, if I may use the language loosely, historians call an interregnum, a period between two reigns. His first 'reign' — good in karts, Brands Festival Champion with a burn from the stern, F3 Champion, the wins in 3000, the big F1 debut in Rio — was over. He'd circle until the second 'reign' began, if it ever did.

Thompson says that 'Johnny did a lot of driving in Japan, which built up his leg muscles and his confidence, although I don't think his confidence was ever that damaged because Johnny's not like

Bending the 1993 Lotus to an Adelaide corner (Formula One Pictures).

that. He always gives 100% — but you go out and try braking with the middle of your foot. He couldn't do it the orthodox way because the strength still wasn't there. He couldn't heel-and-toe properly. So Japan was quite good from that point of view and he got paid reasonably.'

At the tail end of the season he drove twice for Lotus in Grands Prix, replacing regular driver Donnelly who'd been seriously injured in a crash in Spain. Logical: Herbert was, after all, the Lotus test driver. At Suzuka he retired (engine) and at Adelaide he retired (clutch). In December Peter Collins returned to guide Lotus to reclaim its lost heritage, fashion it into a force again; was this the beginning of the second 'reign'? It would be a merciless examination of Herbert's persistence, stamina and optimism.

A strange season, 1991, with Herbert contesting Japanese F3000, Le Mans and, as it happened, Formula 1.

I remember a test session at Imola before the San Marino Grand Prix, Julian Bailey taking the Lotus round, and it was virgin white, no sponsors' logos at all. The reclaiming of the heritage would be hard. Bailey and Hakkinen began the season, but Bailey dropped out after Monaco because his sponsorship had expired and he couldn't bring any more money to the team. That let Herbert in for Canada, but he had mechanical problems and failed to qualify. He did squeeze into the Mexican Grand Prix on the last row of the grid and finished tenth, two laps behind the winner.

A week later he was at Le Mans partnering Volker Weidler and Gachot in a 1.3r Mazda. They'd have to beat the Jaguars and Porsches, and did. I don't want to play down this achievement, but Le Mans is much more about teamwork, reliability and maintaining an even pace than racing in the accepted sense. The teamwork worked, the Mazda was solidly reliable — it ran in the top ten all the way through and made only routine pit stops — while each of the three drivers was eminently capable of keeping the right pace.

However, *Autosport* reported that 'poor Herbert was exhausted after his last and very stressful two-hour stint [to take the car to victory]. It was made harder by the arrival of hot and sunny weather after lunchtime, and he keeled over in his father's arms on climbing out of the car. He was carted off for medical attention and missed the loud and very emotional rostrum celebration.'

After Le Mans he drove another six Grands Prix: 10, 14, 7, retired, retired, 11. Hard.

He did 1992 as a proper, full-time Formula 1 driver again, partnering Hakkinen. By the seventh round, Montreal, he had won a single point (in round one, South Africa). Round the Ile Notre Dame he qualified sixth, and he hadn't been anywhere near that high before in the season. When I tackled him he unconsciously revealed how a driver thinks. 'Qualifying in Montreal was good but I don't want to be sixth, I want to be higher up. The problem for me was the gap from fifth to sixth. It was a second, too big, far, far too big.' Schumacher 1:20.456; Herbert 1:21.645.

We have now reached the point where I turn the wheel and it goes there

---

'We need a bit more testing, we need a bit more [loud into my tape-recorder] SPONSORSHIP. The car has a lot of potential. It's still not right but it's good — and we haven't done any bloody testing. If it had kept going in Canada [the clutch failed] I'd have been on the podium. I've never been depressed. I don't need to be that. Why should I? As soon as we got the new car for the San Marino Grand Prix bang, we were straight back in again.' He also said, 'I'm going to limp for ever. I won't get any — what's the word? — sympathy. I'm walking normally but it's a funny walk, my bum's stuck out, very odd; but my feet are absolutely fine. I have no problems driving the car.'

After Canada he took one more point (in France). Yes, hard.

He did 1993 as a proper, full-time driver and approached it, as did the whole Lotus team, with hope. The new car was launched at a Press Conference at Claridges in London, an occasion of some opulence. Collins said that the car was the one he and Technical Director Peter Wright 'wanted to build when we took over two years ago. It has taken those two years to put in place the necessary research and development.'

Herbert, who had tested it in Portugal, said that 'since I started doing Formula 1 I have always expected a Grand Prix car to do certain things — like a go-kart, really. When you turn the wheel it goes round a corner. If you need a bit more you turn it a bit more and it responds to that. I've always felt we've not quite had that, but the last couple of weeks I feel we have — it isn't twitching and oversteering, which you can get sometimes. I hate the damn things when they do things like that! We have now reached the point where I turn the wheel and it goes there.'

This active suspension, however, would present recurring problems, although Herbert finished fourth in Brazil (after being overtaken by Schumacher and re-taking him instantly) and fourth in the European Grand Prix at Donington. The weather shifted back and forth from wet to not-so-wet to dry to not-so-dry. Lap charts became surreal as cars pitted the whole time for tyres to match the weather — Alain Prost in the Williams seven times. Herbert pitted once, on lap 10, and rode out the storm from there. Everyone remembers Senna's extraordinary victory — at one stage he led by a lap — but how many remember Herbert's extraordinary fourth place?

He finished the season ninth in the Championship with 11 points. He'd give Lotus one more chance.

• CHAPTER FOUR •

The rack

THAT DECEMBER'S DAY in 1993 nothing seemed to have changed. Ketteringham Hall, nestled into the Norfolk slumber, stood solid and stately and timeless. The landscaped gardens, the ponds with their reed beds, the copses of elderly trees proclaimed permanence. The stables nearby, in perfect proportion to the Hall, stood solid too. The Australian Grand Prix was already a memory and the new season — Brazil in March — closing.

Collins, sober-suited and respectable enough to be your bank manager, sat on a leather chair in a reception room that had that musty odour of an old library. He spoke, as people who run racing teams do, of confidence and hope.

'You have what you have and the challenge is there regardless of the amount of money, the amount of resources. If you accept the challenge, you must take the resources you have and maximise them. It's not necessarily the size of the resources, although that helps. There is a cut-off point below which it does hurt, but above that it's how you use them. While ours are significantly smaller than the top four or five teams in pounds per point we've won, we've probably used our resources better with the exception of Williams and McLaren.'

That December Lotus was not as solid as its Ketteringham Hall headquarters, but there was no suggestion that a doomsday scenario was beginning to play itself out; and it wouldn't be accompanied by rolling thunder, but a drip-drip-drip.

I mention that across 1993 there'd been tantalising moments when it looked to be coming right. 'Johnny is a fast racing driver and there's no doubt about it. We've shown flashes of real speed and performance in the last two years. Part of our problem in the last year, I think, has been that we developed an "active" system which — when it worked — more than compensated for any deficiencies in the engine: as evidenced by Monza, where our 600 and whatever-it-was horsepower Cosworth was able to tail Gerhard Berger with his 760 horsepower Ferrari very comfortably.'

Lotus moved into 1994 with Mugen Honda engines and an array of new sponsors — but drip-drip-drip. In early March Collins lambasted McLaren for trying to poach Herbert. 'It's irritating to have another team making clear its interest in a driver who is under contract to you. There is a correct manner in which to deal with these issues. McLaren has not acted in this manner; it has not acted correctly. It was informed by both Johnny and the team of his contractual position, but its subsequent contact with the team has been minimal. It is flattering for Johnny that McLaren should consider him a suitable replacement for Senna [who'd joined Williams], but I am here to look after Team Lotus, not McLaren, so we will be racing this year with Johnny Herbert and Pedro Lamy. Team Lotus has no intention of assisting McLaren in resolving its difficulties.'

Soon enough, Lotus would have difficulties of their own. They took an 'interim' car to Brazil, where Herbert qualified 21st and finished a resolute seventh two laps behind the winner, Schumacher. At the Pacific Grand Prix at Aida, Japan, he qualified 23rd and finished seventh, three laps behind the winner, Schumacher. At Imola he qualified 20th and finished tenth, two laps behind the winner, Schumacher; meaningless across a weekend when a manic, malevolent spirit visited its wrath on Formula 1 — Rubens Barrichello hurt, newcomer Ratzenberger killed, Senna killed, people in the crowd injured, a mechanic run over in the pit lane.

Imola has been explored emotionally and exhaustively enough already; but I do want to talk briefly about how writers who earn their living from motor racing cope with the aftermath. How do you ask a driver about the death of another driver? Have you the right to ask? Are you doing your job if you don't ask? I haven't met anyone who finds these things easy.

Months after Imola I was updating a book on Gerhard Berger (*The Human Face of Formula 1*, PSL) and I'd heard that Berger and Herbert had found a way of attending both funerals, which were on different continents on consecutive days. After that of Senna in Sao Paulo they flew to Brussels, boarded Berger's own plane and continued to Salzburg for that of Ratzenberger. With some trepidation I rang Herbert about this. If he'd sworn at me and put the phone down I couldn't have blamed him.

Moreover, the sensitivity of the whole thing might have been compounded by the fact that Berger had been extremely close to Senna and, in a sense, I'd be inviting Herbert to intrude on Berger's grief — which he had witnessed — by telling me about it, and then I'd tell everybody else about it in the updated book.

As we have seen by now, Johnny Herbert is neither a fool nor insensitive. He spoke in the most straightforward, sensible way. He explained that he felt a moral obligation to go to Senna's funeral and was disappointed that more drivers hadn't felt the same, although he tempered the opinion by conceding that different drivers react to these things in different ways. Overall, however, he believed that it was a matter of showing proper respect whatever your own feelings.

He said he'd competed against Senna in karts as far back as 1982 [the Worlds, Kalmar] and their relationship had been good enough to permit some joking around between them. He explained how in Sao Paulo he fell into conversation with Berger, who mentioned the possibility of getting from Brussels to Salzburg in time. He said how strained that last leg of the journey proved to be, Berger withdrawn far into himself, Herbert unsure whether to try and make polite conversation or let it all go in silence.

They were the words of a man unafraid of the truth.

Genuine Formula 1 chaos followed Imola, with a rush to change rules and a rush by the drivers to have a voice in any changes; and then, at Monaco two weeks later, Karl Wendlinger (Sauber) crashed on the Thursday morning session and was taken to hospital in a coma. Monaco was something to be endured. Herbert qualified 16th and ran ninth towards the end before the gearbox failed.

Between Monaco and Spain, Lotus unveiled its new car, the 109, upon which all hope now lay. In Spain Herbert qualified 22nd and spun after 41 laps. In Canada he qualified 17th and finished eighth, a lap behind the winner, Schumacher. In France he qualified 19th and finished seventh, two laps behind the winner, Schumacher. Drip-drip-drip.

At Silverstone he qualified 18th on the Friday and, during a brief TV interview, explained why the media weren't crowding round him, even though this was the British Grand Prix. *When you're at my end of the grid*, he said — half-grin, half-serious — *nobody wants to know you*. The television channel Eurosport transmitted this early on the Saturday morning and I happened to see it before leaving for Silverstone. Right, I thought, we'll see about that.

There he was on the upper deck of the Lotus motorhome, daughter Chloe — then three — using it as a playground. 'What are you doing here?' he wonders.

'I've come to hold your hand. I can't bear to see you lonely.'

'Oh gawd. What do you really want?'

Smoke but no fire. The Lotus at Imola, 1994 (Formula One Pictures).

'Truly, to keep you company.'

'Nah . . .'

'Truly . . .'

We talked of this and that. By now it must have been apparent to him that the Lotus 109 was almost certainly not the answer, but he didn't communicate anything like *that*. If you're in proximity to him he crackles with life and communicates that. His daughter, meanwhile, is having a drink, risks spilling it down her dress and Herbert is chiding her. 'Be careful, be careful, or mummy will be very cross.'

It's a lovely juxtaposition of the perceived driver's image: boat, beach, blonde. (A few years ago Herbert suddenly interrupted an interview I was doing with him on the phone. 'Got to go now. I'm in the middle of changing nappies.')

At Silverstone he finished 12th, two laps behind the winner, Hill. In Germany he qualified 15th but crashed with Brundle on the opening lap. In Hungary he qualified 24th and dropped out after 34 laps, electrics. He was close to despair.

'I thought, "I can't go on driving a car I don't want to drive." I was feeling that low I wasn't enjoying it. I discussed it with Becky and she said she'd back me up no matter what I decided. I thought I'd enjoy myself more doing British or German Touring Cars.'

In Belgium he qualified 20th and finished 12th, three laps behind the winner, Hill.

I've covered each race for a reason. The results demonstrate the plight of Herbert and Lotus, but also set a context for what happened next. Lotus went to Monza for the Italian Grand Prix with a new Mugen engine, which, in testing at Silverstone, had enabled Herbert to make the car go three seconds quicker; but if you listened carefully you could hear drip-drip-drip. Lotus was on the brink of financial insolvency with debts estimated at £10 million and, as *Autosport* reported, 'Johnny's relationship with Lotus has deteriorated badly throughout the year, to the point where he and team boss Peter Collins have not spoken for much of it.'

The new — lighter — engine delivered a lot of power. On the Friday Herbert had a touch of understeer and complained of problems balancing the car round the Parabolica curve on to the start-finish line, *but* qualified sixth. After all the slow agonies of the season this represented a sensation; and more — Herbert rediscovering the joy of

Conversation with Martin Brundle, Spain 1994 (Formula One Pictures).

being fast and demonstrating that his ability to be fast hadn't gone away.

In the Saturday morning untimed session he carried out some experimenting (well, fine-tuning) for the all-important afternoon second qualifying. Of that qualifying he'd say, 'You start to doubt yourself when all the aggro goes on for too long, and even this afternoon I was getting better and better with every run, braking later and later.' The Lotus looked nimble and quick; and was. For a time, in fact, Herbert was quicker than Hill. The session ended

Alesi (Ferrari)   1:23.844
Berger(Ferrari)   1:23.978
Hill (Williams)   1:24.158
Herbert (Lotus)   1:24.374

Herbert gave a television interview with a completely different tenor from Silverstone. 'My best position so far. Obviously the way things had been going this year was very, very difficult and it's nice that we've got an engine and a good package and it seems to be working.

121

The leaving of Lotus. Herbert joined Ligier for the European Grand Prix at Jerez — his only race for the team (Formula One Pictures).

It would have been nice to stay in front of Damon (naughty smile) but I'll have to get him next time (extended naughty smile).' More privately Herbert confessed that he thought of winning the race, however 'bloody stupid' that may have seemed.

Monza is a rush to the first chicane and a vast compression into the chicane because it's tight, narrow and sharp. At the green light Alesi led the rush, Berger angling over towards him, Hill in mid-track and Herbert angling towards Hill. Approaching the jaws of the chicane, Alesi led with Berger just behind, but it seemed that Herbert held the advantage over Hill and would thread through third. Instead Eddie Irvine (Jordan) — rushing within the rush — got his braking wrong and rammed the Lotus, twisting it, beaching it on the kerbing. The race was stopped, the Lotus too badly damaged to go to the re-start. Herbert would take the re-start from the pit lane in the *old* car with the *old* engine. 'Irvine has done far too much damage this year and should finally be properly penalised. Formula 1 doesn't need drivers like this,' he said. He was 14th when the engine failed.

The day after Monza, Lotus applied for administration, something granted by a court to give a company breathing space from creditors and, by definition, a period of time to try and organise its own salvation. The administration was granted. What Herbert had been able to make the new car do, you see, represented a chance for the salvation. If Lotus maintained progress, kept Mugen Honda engines for 1995 and became a real force again, they'd be very attractive indeed to potential sponsors and maybe a buyer.

Collins and Herbert revealed the width of the gap between them. Collins was quoted as saying, 'At the end of 1993, International Management Group [who handle the affairs of leading sportspersons] latched on to him and wheeled him down to McLaren. They were putting ideas in his head, telling him he should be doing this and that, and that half the paddock was after him — which irritated me immensely because they hadn't been there when nobody wanted him. Then Ron Dennis made him an offer, and Johnny wanted out.

'I told him, "Look, Johnny, if Ron wants you that badly we'll do a deal, but he has to come up with the money." Johnny was saying that he'd been forced to sign the Lotus contract, but I don't think that's fair. I told him, "We agreed it — I've paid you for three years and you haven't brought a penny to the team. You can't expect me to just let you go, even if I'd like to see you going well in a McLaren. I've got shareholders and sponsors who have invested on the back of you being part of the team. I can't just drop them and let you go because it suits you.'"

Collins then spoke more generally, saying that Herbert 'got into the mode of saying the car was undrivable, that there was no future. I think he's had some bad advice and I told him he could do himself a lot of damage by his behaviour. Some people in the paddock saw it as unprofessional.'

Herbert was quoted as saying at Monza, after qualifying fourth: 'When things go well it's always easy to be patting each other on the back, but we haven't really spoken for the past six months. When I've tried to have discussions with him, sometimes it's almost as if he didn't want to listen and I found that very frustrating. He was emotional today. He came back to the van and there were tears in his eyes. For him it's good because he's put a lot of hard work in, but I've got to see how it goes.'

The Benetton launch for the 1995 season (Formula One Pictures).

Perry McCarthy can give a context to the tenor of Herbert's words. We were discussing the mad dog days, and I say I can't imagine Herbert getting drunk.

'Well, he does have a few beers every now and again.'

But not drunk.

'Happy, yes, but not fight-the-world. He's not that type of character. He's not — what's the word? It begins with b . . .'

Boisterous?

'No, it's not that, it's not malicious either, it's . . . belligerent. He's not like that, not belligerent. He's pretty cool. In fact, all the years I've known him I've only seen him angry two or three times. He has a different way of displaying it to somebody like me. I'm kind of fiery, whereas John will be pretty damn quiet and then make a few cutting remarks without a smile on his face — with a dead stare — and that's his way of displaying it, and that's when you know he's angry.

I see other drivers doing well, drivers I know I can beat, and I want the chance to take them on

---

'I've got a theory about John. Believe me, people think that with him everything is water off a duck's back because he just turns around and laughs, and for sure he does do that. In the same situation, myself or Blundell or Bailey would absolutely destroy somebody verbally if they gave us stick or said something stupid. The destruction can create enemies, but we're strong-headed. John would giggle. He'd probably be thinking *you idiot* but he'd let it go because people's actions and comments don't frustrate him to the same degree.

'John's not argumentative. What I never realised is that I'd argue with people and win that immediate battle but lose the war because people lock on to you — *that lippy bastard* or *that flash sod* — and you start getting an image. I'd forget that people in this game gossip more than a WVS social morning. John didn't say much, laughed, had a great sense of humour and that was it. He messed around but even his messing around was never malicious, just very sociable.

'So everybody's interpretation of Johnny is very laid back, the water off the duck's back, lovely chap — because he's not giving it back — but he's been through several different situations, hasn't he?

He had a problem with Mike Thompson, he had a problem with Eddie Jordan at one time, a problem with Peter Collins. Now what that suggests to me is that there is a whole different ball game going on inside which says *we'll be friends and we'll get on well but this is what I want to do and if you step outside that, or if you're not doing enough for me, then we are not going to continue together.* Really, nobody has added those packages and come up with that idea.

'Johnny is very determined and that is not to his detriment, absolutely not. I think in that respect Johnny has been quietly more ruthless than I have. I really do believe that. It might take a while to come to that, because he's not a prima donna at all, but there will be a small build-up of situations where he'll start thinking *this isn't right.*

'The facts of life are that, whatever leads you to a certain position, that position then has to work. This is a ruthless game. Opinions are formed very quickly and changed even quicker. Unless there is a clear progression in a career and unless there is star quality — or even the chance to display star quality — you are going to be rubbished and you won't be spending longer than six months with a team. You have been put under the international spotlight, but you have to make sure you are given the back-up so that the spotlight doesn't melt you . . .'

Portugal, the Grand Prix after Monza, proved crucial. In Friday qualifying Herbert spun and stalled, needed a push start. The stewards disqualified him. On the Saturday he qualified 20th and slogged to 11th, a lap down on the winner, Hill. Herbert had come to the crossroads.

'I don't resent Peter for trying to hang on to me, of course I don't. I understand it from his side. People say I have to repay him and to an extent I agree with them, but the time has come when I have to go my own way and think of myself. I see other drivers doing well, drivers I know I can beat, and I want the chance to take them on. That is why I want to leave. I would love to be with Lotus and make it succeed, I would absolutely love to, but it has not happened and I cannot keep waiting. Our poor performance in Estoril hit me hard. If you put Schumacher in a Lotus he would be in the same position.'

On the Tuesday before the European Grand Prix at Jerez, Herbert signed for the Ligier team and the following day was testing their car at Magny-Cours 'unbeknown to Lotus', *Autosport* reported.

Left *Flavio Briatore, the man running Benetton* (Ford).

'Unbeknown, too, to former Ligier driver Eric Bernard, who was packing his bag to leave for the European Grand Prix when Ligier boss Cesare Fiorio phoned and told him to report to the Lotus bus when he arrived in Jerez!'

Ligier was owned by Flavio Briatore, the boss of Benetton, and there were suggestions that if Benetton needed points in the Constructors' Championship they might commandeer Herbert to support Schumacher. Neither of Schumacher's partners — J. J. Lehto and Jos Verstappen — had been able to lend him much of that thus far, Lehto six races for 1 point, Verstappen nine races for 10 points.

At Jerez Herbert qualified seventh (his team-mate Olivier Panis 11th) and drove conservatively to eighth. Inevitably he was asked to compare the Lotus and Ligier. 'Night and day.'

In the Constructors' table Benetton led Williams 97–95, and in the Championship Schumacher led Hill 86–81. Briatore examined the forces at his disposal for the last two races and set Herbert to testing the Benetton at Barcelona. He went off into the gravel almost immediately, but subsequently got to within 0.4 seconds of Schumacher's best time. His career at Ligier was over. He'd drive Japan and Australia in the Benetton.

In Japan he qualified within 0.61 seconds of Schumacher, and neither Lehto nor Verstappen had been that close. The race was filthy wet and he ran third when Heinz-Harald Frentzen (Sauber) skimmed off. On lap 3, emerging from the chicane, Herbert felt the Benetton 'wiggle'. He used the accelerator gently but the car was spinning 'like a top', *and* the pits were calling over the radio that the safety car was coming out. If he'd known this one second earlier, he estimated, it would have altered everything. He'd have backed off completely. As it was, aquaplaning, he went helplessly into the wall.

While Schumacher was winning the Championship in Adelaide, Herbert retired after 13 laps, gearbox.

He was confirmed as Benetton's number two driver for 1995 in late January and said (ominously, as it proved), 'I hear what people say about the car being set up around Michael, and obviously it's going to be, but I don't think there's that much in set-up.' Herbert approached 1995 'full of confidence that finally I had the chance I had been looking for since my first Grand Prix' — a winning car. The comparison with Schumacher had always been daunting for his team-mates.

1992 Schumacher 53 Brundle 38
1993 Schumacher 52 Patrese 20
1994 Schumacher 92 Lehto 1, Verstappen 10, Herbert 0

Herbert's confidence grew in Brazil, the opening race. He didn't get a qualifying run on the Friday — Schumacher crashed heavily and Herbert wasn't allowed out until they located the cause — but on the Saturday Herbert finished 'very pleased', not far behind the Williamses of Hill and David Coulthard.

Schumacher 1:20.382
Coulthard 1:20.422
Hill 1:20.429
Herbert 1:20.888

Reviewing this, and surely hinting that Schumacher wanted to establish an immediate tone, Herbert would say that 'it wasn't as if I was expecting him [Schumacher] to be nice as pie and help me. In a way, why should he? He's the World Champion, the number one driver, and if I was giving him a hard time he'd lose his aura. In Brazil I was quicker than him in the last part of qualifying and he had the [trace] sheets out looking to see where. I expected that.'

In the race Herbert was engulfed at the green light, lost more places with a spin and eventually retired after a slight collision with Aguri Suzuki (Ligier).

On the Friday in Argentina

Schumacher (ninth) 1:57.056
Herbert (tenth) 1:57.068

On the Saturday

Schumacher (third) 1:54.272
Herbert (13th) 1:57.341

'Nobody is that much slower than their team-mate in Formula 1,' Herbert would say. 'That is when I began to feel that I wasn't completely part of things, that Michael had some set-up information or components that I didn't have access to. The team was adamant that that wasn't the case, so I don't suppose we'll ever know.' He finished the race fourth.

At Imola the gap opened again on the Friday, Schumacher 1:27.274 (provisional pole), Herbert 1:29.403 (eighth). Next day Herbert improved but only marginally, to 1:29.350. 'Michael was quicker than me nearly everywhere,' Herbert said. 'That's unusual because I'm often slower than him in slow sections, but it was absolutely everywhere, which was surprising.' He finished seventh, two laps down on the winner, Hill, and someone noted that 'he and engineer Tim Wright appear to be left to their own devices. Frustration is starting to creep in.'

The major frustration was that the Benetton had been designed to suit Schumacher's style, and setting it up was governed by that. The car 'was very, very twitchy,' Herbert says. 'That was the biggest thing with it. At times — when I said to myself *I've got to push it* — it would go straight off the circuit. It was never forgiving in any sort of

The podium at the fourth race of 1995, Spain (Formula One Pictures).

way. Michael had a different style and it worked for him very well, but when someone else drove it in a different way it made it much more difficult. One moment the car was on the limit, the next you'd overstepped it and you were spinning. That suited Michael's style, and because he was the team's lead drive there was no incentive to change it.

'I think they realised, but because Michael was in the team there was not a lot they could change. Maybe it was better their way — they were going for the Championship. I've always felt that I should be able to drive any sort of car, and you can criticise J. J. Lehto and a few others when they were at Benetton, but when you handled the car you saw how difficult it could be.'

Another frustration was lack of testing. 'I was never given the time to test and sort it out my way, so I was always trying to catch up at the races. That's not the place to do it.' A further frustration was uncertainty over whether he would be retained for 1996. *Autosport* caught that mood just after Imola. 'Benetton has denied that Herbert has just an eight-race deal, but Verstappen is under contract to Benetton boss Flavio Briatore and could be brought back to the team at any time.'

'Looking back,' Herbert says, 'probably the hardest thing was the constant feeling *this is my last race*. I got that so early and it just seemed to go on and on and on up until after Silverstone [the eighth race]. Then it died down and never came back. It was just so stupid because the rumour had to come from somewhere. It wasn't something that just suddenly turned up. Somebody had to say something. At the time I didn't feel I felt it, but I think I did really. It wasn't a nice thing to have hanging over you all the time.'

Paradoxically, at the next race, Spain, Schumacher — under pressure from spinning off at Imola — took pole again and the team said, 'We have to give Johnny a lot of credit for helping us to arrive at the set-up we did.' Paradox? Herbert, on the fourth row, was two seconds slower again. At the green light Herbert was in mid-pack and, as they strung out through the loops at the end of the straight, ran eighth. He emerged from the second rush of pit stops fifth, although the emerging was bizarre: he set off with the jack still under the back of the car! The jack came off all by itself at the far end of the pit lane. Schumacher led from Hill, Coulthard third, Herbert fourth, but

The Brits at Silverstone. From left: Coulthard, Hill, Herbert, Eddie Irvine, Brundle, Blundell (ICN UK Bureau).

Coulthard retired — gearbox — and Hill drove the last lap crippled by a gearbox problem, making Herbert second. It was the best result of his Formula 1 career, but it was also 51.988 seconds behind Schumacher.

A familiar scene at Monaco, Schumacher front row, Herbert fourth row, Schumacher winning, Herbert fourth a lap behind. In Canada (Schumacher pole, Herbert third row) he and Hakkinen collided at the hairpin on the opening lap, Herbert rightly angry; in France (Schumacher front row, Herbert fifth row) he was tapped by Alesi and spun out almost immediately. 'He seemed to do such a silly move — well, it wasn't even a move because he didn't try to go up the inside, he tapped my back wheel and it just spun me round.'

This cost Herbert money, and for a convoluted reason. In 1995 an electronic eye was being used to gauge if any driver jumped the start, something controversial because the eye was so sensitive that *any* movement seemed to trigger it and many a driver disputed that they'd been in motion at all. The eye had judged that Herbert jumped the start in Canada, bringing a 10-second stop-go penalty — which, clearly, he hadn't been able to serve because he crashed with Hakkinen before he could. He received a $10,000 suspended fine. Now in France the eye said he'd jumped the start again — but he'd crashed with Alesi after two laps, again not enough time to serve the sentence. The stewards fined him the $10,000 from Canada . . .

Was it only the year before that Herbert had been at Lotus and so lonely at Silverstone, of all places for a Briton, that people weren't bothering to talk to him?

He qualified on the third row next to Alesi (Schumacher on the front row) and ran fifth, largely unnoticed because Alesi made a tumult of a start, spearing down the inside to thrust in behind Hill but in front of Schumacher. The immediate order was Hill, Alesi, Schumacher, Coulthard, Herbert, with these time gaps to Hill crossing the line to complete lap 1:

Alesi	at 1.171
Schumacher	at 1.828
Coulthard	at 2.424
Herbert	at 3.335
Hakkinen	at 3.950

The core of the race, bearing in mind the Championship, was Hill versus Schumacher. Around Silverstone's broad acres Alesi acted as a temporary spoiler, loading pressure on to Schumacher who needed to overtake to get at Hill and couldn't. Again largely unnoticed, Hakkinen accelerated, squeezing Herbert a bit.

Coulthard pitted on lap 16, making Herbert fourth, but it didn't seem to mean much. Alesi pitted next, making Herbert third. He made his own stop on lap 21 — stationary for 10.1 seconds — and got out in front of Alesi. He held third nicely to lap 40 when he made his second stop, losing the place to Coulthard but regaining it three laps later when Coulthard pitted. The pit stops — here and everywhere else — tended to make the true structure of a race elusive. Order: Hill, Schumacher, Herbert, Coulthard.

A dramatic instant on the way to winning the Italian Grand Prix (ICN UK Bureau).

On lap 40 Herbert made his second stop, giving Coulthard the third place. On lap 41 Hill made his second stop, giving Schumacher the lead. On lap 43 Coulthard made his second stop, giving the third place back to Herbert. The structure had been established for the run to the end: Hill charging at Schumacher, Coulthard charging at Herbert. After 44 laps the time gaps from Schumacher were:

Hill   at 0.496
Herbert   at 47.036
Coulthard   at 51.058

On lap 45 Hill and Schumacher crashed. The circumstances are relevant to Herbert's story only in the effect they had. The rights and wrongs of the crash need not concern us here. While Hill clambered out of the Williams and Schumacher clambered out of the Benetton and both walked across the gravel trap where their cars had come to rest, Herbert went by — leading the British Grand Prix.

Coulthard swarmed, wanting that lead for himself. Under Bridge and into Priory — the 'complex' of corners before the start-finish straight — Coulthard tried a lunge down the inside but Herbert repulsed it. At exactly that moment Coulthard was given a 10-second stop-go penalty for speeding in the pit lane during his last stop . . .

At Stowe, Coulthard made another move, jinking right to the inside and, although they almost stroked wheels, Herbert let him go. 'They told me on the radio about the 10-second penalty before David came up to pass me,' Herbert said, 'and that took away a lot of the pressure, of course.' Coulthard came in to serve his time, the race gone from him.

Herbert described the final ten laps as 'incredible'. He felt the power of the sea of Union Jacks waving so urgently to him in triumphal ripples all round the circuit, but you don't surrender to emotion. *Hang, on, hang on,* he told himself, *you've been doing this long enough to know that anything can happen.*

He crossed the line 16.479 seconds in front of Alesi.

It was the most popular win in the world.

Many months later, from the quietness of memory, Herbert evaluated the race with candour. 'There was always this *oh well, I was lucky, I was in the right place and all the others fell off.* I was third when Damon and Michael fell off so, sure, I was there at the right time, but also I was more competitive than I had been. Then you look at the situation with David. I didn't have to worry about him, and that made it a lot easier on me.'

Even after the win, rumours suggested that he'd be replaced by Verstappen although at the time Herbert said (typically), 'I haven't heard anything about them throwing me out. As far as I'm concerned, I'm in for the year.'

Briatore explained that Herbert had a contract to the end of the season [which is not the same thing as driving every race until the end of the season] and commented, 'I handle the team in the way I believe is right, and if he gets results he will be in the car.' Whether uncertainty is a good incentive in Formula 1 depends on how you view man-management. No doubt in some circumstances it acts as a stimulant, but I believe that, if it is sustained over a period, it becomes destructive; and it is entirely the wrong approach with Johnny Herbert in all circumstances.

In Germany Schumacher kept the two-second qualifying chasm and in the race Herbert had throttle problems but came fourth. In

Hungary Schumacher kept the chasm; and in the race Herbert battled to fourth a whisker behind Berger's Ferrari. He now stood fifth in the World Championship.

It was August, high season for who's-going-where-for-1996 stories, of which there were a whole harvest: Schumacher to Ferrari for $25 million a year, Alesi to Benetton, Barrichello or Frentzen to partner Alesi, Jacques Villeneuve from IndyCars to Williams, Coulthard or Berger to McLaren. Nobody talked much about Herbert, although Tom Walkinshaw, Benetton's engineering director, was quoted as being critical of Herbert's approach ('Johnny does not seem to want to apply himself to winning races at the top level' and more in the same vein). I understand that what Walkinshaw said was taken out of context and not meant in the way it appeared, but the fact that it appeared in any form seemed somehow significant.

Easy to forget that, departing Hungary, Herbert had 28 points. In the whole of 1994 Verstappen and Lehto scored 11 between them; in the whole of 1993 Patrese scored 20; only Brundle's 38 in 1992 surpassed what Herbert had already done, and Herbert had seven

Digging smoke in Portugal (Formula One Pictures).

races left to score more. Since 1992 *only* Schumacher had won a race for Benetton until Herbert at Silverstone.

Spa was a revelation, literally and unfortunately.

In the Friday morning untimed session — moist and murky, of course — Herbert emerged from La Source hairpin, lost control, thumped the barrier and performed three 360-degree spins. 'All I know is the data says it was 12G impact,' he said. 'You black out at 8G so I don't remember much. It was a big impact. I got out and was wobbling around as if I was drunk. If I shake my head it still hurts. I don't recall how I got to the medical centre — I was on another planet. It was a very strange accident. I had a bit of wheelspin, put on opposite lock and it just went straight into the barrier.' Although he was medically fit to drive in the afternoon, the car could not be repaired in time, spare cars weren't permitted and Benetton did not countenance the idea of Herbert sharing Schumacher's car. He had to watch the session.

In the Saturday morning untimed session Schumacher crashed, the car could not be repaired in time (but the mechanics were working hard on it), and Benetton wouldn't let Herbert out in case Schumacher needed his car. That was the revelation. 'I was very pleased with my laps when I got out, but I was a bit annoyed that there was some confusion earlier and neither of us got out.' Herbert was being extremely diplomatic, let us say. In the race he finished seventh.

After Spa Berger announced he'd be joining Benetton for 1996. Herbert was out and Herbert was not happy. He described Schumacher as 'the most selfish driver I have ever worked with', and added, 'He was happy enough to choose me as a partner but when he realised I could drive quickly our friendship changed. He saw me as a threat and he didn't like it.'

At Monza Herbert spoke of feeling like an 'outcast'. Schumacher said, 'I can't really believe this is coming from my team-mate', and Briatore murmured that Herbert 'knew what to expect when he joined us. I don't tell Johnny how to drive a car and I don't expect him to tell me how to run the team.' Happy families . . .

Right *By the Pacific Grand Prix at Aida the relationship with Benetton was soured* (Formula One Pictures).

Herbert qualified eighth, the chasm 1.5 seconds to Schumacher on the front row, while Monza prepared to surrender to the emotion of Alesi and Berger's last races for Ferrari there. At the green light Herbert made what he'd describe as a 'perfect' start, and that allowed him to jerk to mid-track for the rush to the chicane, but a multiple accident stopped the whole thing. At the re-start he got away well again and the order completing lap 1 was Coulthard, Berger, Schumacher, Hill, Alesi, Herbert.

Barrichello nipped by Herbert and so did Hakkinen, none of which worried him unduly with 50 laps remaining. On lap 13 Coulthard spun off, cranking everyone up a place — Herbert seventh. On lap 23 Hill and Schumacher collided, cranking Herbert up to fifth. Order: Berger, Alesi, Barrichello, Hakkinen, Herbert. The concentration of pit stops played itself out within five laps, and Herbert led for a couple until he made his own. After 32 laps Alesi led from Berger at 1.247, Herbert at 9.173.

I still think I'm in contention for the Championship

Within two laps Berger was out. An onboard camera broke loose from Alesi's car and smacked into Berger's like a bullet, deranging the left front suspension. Herbert was 8.390 seconds behind Alesi and pushed, cutting the gap to about 6 seconds; but he'd confess that really he'd 'settled for second place'. With only six laps left 'I could see Jean ahead of me, and then coming out of the Lesmo I noticed there was smoke from his car.' Herbert watched Alesi slow, peel off into the pits. 'I knew the gap behind me was a good one, so it was a very pleasant surprise.' Herbert went by in the lead.

The team came on the radio to tell him to preserve the brakes (and keep calm!). He backed off and did what he terms the 'sportscar stuff', meaning you run smoothly and carefully to the end. At the end he said he was wearing the same underpants he'd worn at Silverstone and would be wearing them again . . .

Many months later, from the quietness of memory, Herbert evaluated this race with candour. 'Monza? Sure a lot of people went off but I did set second fastest lap of the race [Berger 1:26.419, Herbert

1:26.481], so I was performing a lot better. If other drivers had won that race, people would have said *oh, fantastic*, and the knowledge of that made it difficult, but I knew I had done the best I possibly could. I felt a lot of relief. Winning the first one is the most difficult. When I won Monza it was a hell of a lot easier, and you know what's going to happen so that side of it helps. Psychologically nothing changed that much because I was still in the same situation' — namely, without a drive for 1996.

The Championship might have been tilting, too — Schumacher 66, Hill 51, but Herbert third on 38. With five races remaining he could overhaul Hill, or more ambitiously overhaul Schumacher as well. 'I still think I'm in contention for the Championship. I could be there at the end.'

Instead it ebbed away, seventh in Portugal and fifth in the European Grand Prix at the Nurburgring. Schumacher duly confirmed the Championship by winning the Pacific Grand Prix at Aida, Herbert sixth. Thence, third in the Japanese Grand Prix and a strong showing in Australia — running second — before the drive-shaft failed. Schumacher 102, Hill 69, Coulthard 49, Herbert 45, Alesi 42, Berger 31.

A few days after Adelaide Berger introduced himself to the Benetton car in testing at Estoril and crashed at 120 mph when, evidently, the car hit a bump. A couple of weeks later it happened again.

By then the BBC had screened a tribute to Schumacher. During it they gave comparative data from qualifying at the British Grand Prix in graph form — throttle, speed, braking, steering — and in each Schumacher seemed superior.

Subsequently Herbert was asked if he felt let down that it had been made public.

'No. They [Benetton] could pluck out any data they wanted. They could have made it as bad as possible or as good as possible. It all depends what it was — it could have been a coming-in lap for all I know! It doesn't bother me whatsoever. The thing that has made me feel a lot better is the problems Gerhard's had. I've only to look at that and I don't feel bad about what happened last year — because I know someone who is as good as Gerhard has had very similar problems; probably, in fact, had it worse, because he's crashed it. That's made me feel a lot more confident.'

141

Did you start to doubt yourself?

'To some degree, but then when I looked at the data there was a massive difference which was unexplainable sometimes.'

How do you regard Benetton now you've left?

'What I will remember most is that nagging sense of frustration, and the regret that voicing some of my concerns — which I felt I needed to do in order to rescue my reputation and ensure that people could understand what was going on — made some of them think I was a whinger. I've never been that in my entire career.' Quite the reverse, and shortly after he was doing some charity work, which I covered for a magazine. This is what I wrote:

'Fog lay static across the circuit, cold enough to numb, dense enough to mask the groups of people who kept melting and dispersing and returning. Silverstone on a winter's day. Somewhere within this fog,

Digging dust in Japan (Formula One Pictures).

engines put-put-puttered and helmets — ghostly, almost — bob-bob-bobbed.

Could that be Damon Hill over there? Yes. And David Coulthard? Yes. And, wait a minute, wait a minute, little Johnny Herbert? Yes. These drivers and others were taking on The Great British Public to raise funding for the Grand Prix Mechanics Charitable Trust. Pay £150 and you got three kart races against celebrities.

'It's the humanity of our sport,' a former driver, John Watson, said. 'It's the human face of our sport.' That's only one aspect among many. Herbert finished fourth in the World Championship, but, this winter's day, has no drive for 1996.

Could it really have been such a short time before, at this same Silverstone in high summer, that he'd won the British Grand Prix? Not to mention the Italian at Monza seven weeks later? And how could it be that Ferrari would hire his team-mate, Michael Schumacher, for $25 million? How could it be that Herbert, a very good competitor, was valued at nothing by Formula 1 and Schumacher valued at more than all the other drivers put together?

Herbert, chirpy and approachable and exchanging banter with autograph hunters, has a smile to penetrate fog, but this winter's day he seemed morose about the future. 'I've not had a happy year,' he said, meaning — despite the two wins — trouble with Schumacher, trouble with Benetton and now virtual rejection.

He talked of IndyCars in the States and insisted he wouldn't settle for a Formula 1 ride just to be in Formula 1.

To the casual tele-spectator all this is extremely mysterious, illogical and inexplicable. So is the fact that about two-thirds of the drivers on any Grand Prix grid are paying to be there. One Brit (Julian Bailey) sold his pub for a chance. Another (Perry McCarthy) mortgaged his house.

It works like this: sponsors, mindful of the massive television exposure (F1 is only behind the World Cup and the Olympics) are prepared to pay very large sums to be with successful teams. It is a perpetuating cycle and very hard to break into. From 1988, to take a random year, there have been 129 Grands Prix. Either Williams, McLaren, Benetton or Ferrari have won the lot.

The middle and lower ranking teams are engaged in a constant struggle to find sponsors — who, of course, won't be paying as much

Moving towards third place in Japan (Formula One Pictures).

— and insist that drivers raise their own money to buy the drive. Half a million dollars will do for starters.

Most British companies, as Frank Williams attests, are coy of any involvement. British drivers have to get there on merit and unless they can raise their careers to a very high plateau — as Nigel Mansell did — they remain vulnerable.

Ask Johnny Herbert.

A couple of anecdotes about the day. Herbert finished his karting stint and set off limp-hobble-wobble — his own method of motion — into the fog, me pursuing because I needed a favour. As it happened, I'd a recurring problem with a vein in one leg and, after a few strides, I couldn't keep up. He began to look quizzical. It must have been the very first time since Brands Hatch on 21 August 1988 that he'd out-walked anyone. Anyway, he was in a hurry, which is what Formula 1 drivers always are, and compounding that he's due in London that same evening (ironically) to talk about the Benetton car — which also will be present — at the BBC Sports Personality of the Year awards. I wanted him to sign a copy of a book [for another

charity]. 'Sure, I'll be coming up to the Media Centre before I leave.'
He hobble-wobbled doggedly onwards until the fog swallowed him.

There is an immutable rule about Formula 1 drivers, aside from
them always being in a hurry, which is that wherever you want them
to be, or wherever they said they will be, *they will be somewhere else.*
This is not necessarily anti-social or being evasive, rather that a
maelstrom of activity follows them round — handshakes, autographs,
photos requests, interviews, old friends looming, and so on, on and
on. The chances, therefore, of Herbert actually coming to the Media
Centre seem remote, even if he remembers he was supposed to be
going there anyway.

This day the Centre is being used as the co-ordinating point for
those who have paid to race the celebrities, one of those rare occasions when you can feel happiness as ordinary folk discover that the
famous are very much like themselves. Someone claimed to have
beaten Herbert at the karting and was enormously proud of this, not
least that Herbert was matey and chatty. And then the occasion got
much rarer.

Herbert arrived!

'There. Told you I was coming.' He signed the book, although, like
many celebrities accustomed to fast-signing, his signature had degen-
erated into something only distantly resembling handwriting. A
couple of fans nearby wanted a word and he obliged; and they in their
turn were clearly astonished at the mateyness and chattiness that
they must have heard about but didn't think could really exist to the
degree it does.

Then he was gone, gone back into the fog and the journey to
London and lengthy television exposure in front of many, many
millions. I watched the BBC Awards that night carefully. He treated
the occasion exactly the same as he had treated the two fans, by
being entirely himself.

Within weeks of this he'd pop up in a theatre in Switzerland,
wreathed in multi-coloured laser beams and smoke, surrounded by
men in armour, and he'd be sitting atop a Formula 1 car singing.
After everything that had gone before in the career, we shouldn't
have been surprised, and maybe we weren't — but, more to the point,
the career was saved.

• CHAPTER FIVE •

Rebirth?

THE SAUBER TEAM was a chance to stay in the mainstream of Formula 1, although the launch of their new car made me wonder. It took place in that theatre outside Zurich and involved an auditorium with a stage, a theatrical troupe, much chanting; and the laser display that was like being transported to another universe. The climax, naturally, was the appearance (on the stage) of the car — the troupe singing lustily and Herbert's lips moving in time with the music. 'I wasn't miming,' he said, 'I was singing, I was doing it properly!'

Enacting the ritual of a car launch — even one like this — demands that all present make optimistic noises; sometimes the optimism is guarded, but it is still there, necessary and tangible. At this point it is extremely difficult to know how the car and the season will go, although there are indications: what happened the previous season (Sauber won 18 points, seventh in the table), which engine this season (Ford), which drivers (Frentzen, Herbert). Beyond that, you have to wait and see.

At Zurich, Herbert was asked — yet again — about how he'd summarise his time at Benetton. 'There were some happy times but probably they were earlier on. There were things that kept hanging over my head, very, very unnecessary things that just made it worse.' And: 'There was something Michael Schumacher wrote last week about when I joined the team I was a really nice guy, one of the nicest, and then I turned out to be one of the horrible ones, but I didn't really see it that way. I had nothing against Michael whatsoever, more that it wasn't a team feeling. I felt a little bit left out.'

After seven years in Formula 1, do you find that each season you have to re-motivate yourself? Do you have to take a new mental attitude? And is it a bigger jump this season than it has been in the past?

'No, it's not a bigger jump. I think it was a bigger jump in 1995 because it was from nothing to a big team. In a way I have made a step back, but hopefully from that step back I can make a step forward. At the same time, I don't feel I have to change, particularly the way I am. You learn from the experiences and I hope I have learned from 1995. The fitness side is something that you have to do: you *have* to make yourself as physically fit as you can and that helps you psychologically. Someone who just trains a bit doesn't have that psychological edge.

'When you join a team, you have to establish at the beginning how it will be and how it will continue. If you go in there weak you will be weak the whole time. If you go in there trying hard and saying "I want to be strong and we want to work together", then it will be

Hard mid-season 1996 — the Sauber's gearbox electronics failed at Hockenheim (Formula One Pictures).

more positive. It was the problem I had at Benetton. I couldn't quite squeeze in there.'

Someone (I can't remember who): *You're the best-looking driver. Have you been on a special course or something?*

'Are you saying I was ugly before? Maybe it's that new tan cream I got for Christmas . . .'

Of Sauber, Herbert expressed delight that they had made him feel one of the team and — yes — he uttered the optimistic noises. Pre-season testing can be misleading for a variety of reasons, so you only discover how prophetic the optimistic noises are when you get to the first race.

That was Melbourne, Australia in March. Frentzen qualified on the fifth row but Herbert, who confessed he'd made a 'balls' of setting his car up, only the seventh. It set a pattern, as it generally does: during 1996 the best Herbert and Frentzen could hope was to be midfield runners picking up what they could. And what Herbert picked up in Melbourne was immediate disappointment — he was involved in a multiple crash on the opening lap. Frentzen had stopped on the parade lap with an electrical fault and now, the race started, the cars streamed into a right-hander. David Coulthard veered across to the left — he said later another car had tapped his McLaren — and, slewing, cannoned against Herbert. Martin Brundle was immediately behind and his Jordan launched over Coulthard and Herbert, landed on its nosecone and skimmed horrifically off upside down.

Herbert's car was too damaged to take the re-start and Frentzen had the spare. Herbert would have to watch.

In Brazil, Frentzen qualified on the fifth row, Herbert the sixth. The electrics failed after 28 laps. In Argentina, Frentzen qualified on the sixth row, Herbert the ninth. In the race he had only front brakes for the last 20 laps and slogged to ninth a lap behind the winner, Hill. The matrix of the season seemed confirmed: midfield runners. And further confirmed in the European Grand Prix at the Nurburgring, Frentzen on the fifth row, Herbert the sixth and slogging to seventh place; continued through the San Marino Grand Prix at Imola (Frentzen the fifth row, Herbert the eighth and retired after 25 laps with a misfire).

Monaco seemed to be more of the same, Frentzen on the fifth row and Herbert the seventh. He had a suspension problem going for a time: 'I felt it sit down and begin to crab. I went through the second intermediate and my time was still up on my best. That's what's so disappointing.' He was a whisker quicker than Olivier Panis (Ligier).

As everybody knows (or thinks they know), grid positions at maddening Monte Carlo are decisive because the track is too tight and taut to overtake. Everything turns on who gets to the first corner first. After that it's follow-my-leader for 75 laps. A wet race — which would mean a duration of two hours because the scheduled 78 laps wouldn't be completed in less than the necessary two hours — and Hill led from Schumacher, although Jos Verstappen (Footwork) — who'd been on the row in front of Herbert — went off at the first corner and Schumacher punted a wall further round. Herbert completed this lap ninth and remained there for a further eight laps when Gerhard Berger (Benetton) had a gearbox problem. Frentzen, meanwhile — aggressive, eager — was up to fourth and by now of the 21 drivers who set off nine had retired. Frentzen harried the Ferrari of Eddie Irvine for third place.

With Herbert running a comfortable eighth, Frentzen harried Irvine too hard, bumped Irvine's rear and broke the Sauber's front wing. Frentzen pitted and that lifted everyone behind a place — Herbert to seventh, of course. On lap 25 Panis got by and after the rush of pit stops between laps 28 and 30 for dry tyres Herbert ran sixth. Order: *Hill, Alesi, Irvine, Panis, Coulthard, Herbert.* Panis hustled Irvine and, at the Loews hairpin, elbowed him aside. *Hill, Alesi, Panis, Coulthard, Herbert.*

On lap 40 Hill, leading by a commanding distance, suddenly had smoke seeping from the back of his Williams in the tunnel, and it became a plume down the incline to the chicane. He thundered along the escape road, stopped, got out and wandered off lost in sudden sadness. *Alesi, Panis, Coulthard, Herbert.* Alesi led Panis by 28.550 seconds, the second win of his career beckoning. The order of the first four endured for 13 laps — then Alesi pitted. The Benetton's suspension had a problem. *Panis, Coulthard, Herbert.*

At this point — lap 54 of what would be 75 — only ten cars remained, soon reduced when Alesi finally gave up and Luca Badoer (Forti) sandwiched Jacques Villeneuve (Williams) against the barrier at the right before Loews; and much further reduced when Irvine lost control after Loews, Mika Salo (Tyrrell) rammed him and Mika Hakkinen (McLaren) rammed Salo.

At this point — lap 71 — only four cars remained. *Panis, Coulthard, Herbert, Frentzen.* And Frentzen calmly pulled in to the pits rather than bother to cover the final lap, knowing he would be classified fourth because nobody remained to catch him . . .

Panis	2h 00m 45.629s
Coulthard	at 4.828s
Herbert	at 37.503s
	and that was it.

In a television interview, Herbert said: 'We still need to improve a hell of a lot engine-wise and with the car but I think we are making small steps. Obviously we want to make it quicker.'

That didn't happen, although Herbert out-qualified Frentzen for the first time at the Spanish Grand Prix (fifth row against sixth). 'I've had a good amount of testing recently, which has helped me get a better rhythm. The chassis is fine in the fast corners but struggles a bit with understeer in the medium and slow ones.' In the race, extremely wet, he spun off. Frentzen out-qualified Herbert in Canada, where Herbert slogged to seventh; out-qualified him in France, where Herbert slogged to eleventh and was disqualified from even there because of a technical infringement.

The return to Silverstone was muted, even in the media previews (which can be extremely chauvinistic), as if everyone understood that the emotional and wondrous conjunction of circumstances that produced 1995 wouldn't be happening again; and they did not. He qualified a row behind Frentzen (sixth against seventh) and slogged to ninth a lap behind the winner, Villeneuve. In Germany he qualified just behind Frentzen (although in this matter Frentzen led 10-1 over the season) and retired after 25 laps with a gearbox problem.

Muted? Yes, because somehow 1996 reflected my feeling about the whole career: it reads like a story with a wonderful (and improbable) beginning, a highly promising (and painful) middle, but little shape and structure to the phase after that — which should have been years of plenty in Formula 1 and were not. It reads like a mystery story, with a twist you didn't see coming at the end of each chapter. What you can say is that the central character still limps, is still irreverent, still keeps a naughty grin available so the steel behind the smile isn't easy to see, and still nurses a profound belief in himself as he awaits the next twist.

• APPENDIX •

Johnny Herbert's career statistics

P = pole; FL = fastest lap; DIS = disqualified; DNQ = did not qualify; DNS = did not start; R = retired.

KARTS

In the late 1970s and early 1980s Herbert competed virtually every weekend and therefore we give only the very highlights, both in 1982: he won the British Senior 135cc Championship and was classified 18th in the World Championships at Kalmar, Sweden.

CARS

1983 Van Diemen 1600cc

28–30 Oct	Formula Ford Festival, Brands Hatch	
	Heat	5
	Quarter-finals	R

1984 Sparton-Ford 1600cc. Championships: BP, Dunlop

4 Mar	Brands Hatch (BP)	6
1 July	Brands Hatch (Dunlop)	3
15 July	Cadwell Park (Dunlop)	5

28 July	Oulton Park (Dunlop)	R
11 Aug	Oulton Park (BP)	4
19 Aug	Brands Hatch (Dunlop)	5
2 Sept	Silverstone (BP)	1
8 Sept	Oulton Park (BP)	3
16 Sept	Snetterton (BP)	5
30 Sept	Mallory Park (Dunlop)	P/3

Dunlop-Autosport *'Star of Tomorrow'*: *J. Bancroft 96, M. Blundell 84, M. Wright 73 (Herbert sixth, 24)*
BP 'Superfind': J. Bancroft 88, M. Blundell 60, E. O'Brien 39 (Herbert eighth, 19)

1985 Quest 1600cc. Championships: RAC, Esso, EFDA Euroseries

3 Mar	Silverstone (Esso)	P/3
17 Mar	Silverstone (RAC)	2
24 Mar	Silverstone (Esso)	FL/2
5 Apr	Oulton Park (RAC)	2
8 Apr	Silverstone (RAC)	R
8 Apr	Silverstone (Esso)	2
6 May	Silverstone (Esso)	R
11 May	Silverstone (Esso)	R
27 May	Thruxton (RAC)	P/4
9 June	Silverstone (RAC)	R
23 June	Snetterton (Esso)	DIS
7 July	Brands Hatch (Esso)	R
14 July	Brands Hatch (RAC)	P/2
14 July	Brands Hatch (EFDA)	P/FL/1
4 Aug	Cadwell Park (Esso)	FL/R
11 Aug	Snetterton (RAC)	3
17 Aug	Oulton Park (Esso)	FL/2
26 Aug	Brands Hatch (RAC)	R
31 Aug	Oulton Park (RAC)	2
8 Sept	Silverstone (Esso)	R
14 Sept	Castle Combe (RAC)	8
29 Sept	Zolder (Euro Final)	R
6 Oct	Brands Hatch (RAC)	R
13 Oct	Silverstone (Esso)	2

| 20 Oct | Thruxton (RAC) | R |
| 27 Oct | Formula Ford Festival, Brands Hatch | 1 |

Esso: M. Blundell 151, A. King 126, D. Hill 119 (Herbert fifth, 97)
RAC: B. Gachot 146, M. Blundell 139, P. Carcasci 125
(Herbert eighth, 70)

1986 Quest-Ivey in the Racing Displays British Formula Ford 2000 to 16 March, then Quest-Nelson; Quest-Ivey in RAC FF1600; Ralt-VW in the Lucas British Formula 3 Championship and Cellnet Superprix. All FF2000 except where stated

9 Mar	Thruxton	R
16 Mar	Silverstone	13
23 Mar	Cadwell Park	9
28 Mar	Oulton Park	R
31 Mar	Thruxton	9
13 Apr	Snetterton	R
27 Apr	Brands Hatch	10
5 May	Castle Combe	R
25 May	Brands Hatch	6
29 June	Snetterton	4
12 July	Brands Hatch (FF1600)	5
20 July	Donington (F3)	5
3 Aug	Brands Hatch (Cellnet F3)	3
10 Aug	Brands Hatch	5
23 Aug	Brands Hatch	10
25 Aug	Silverstone (F3)	4
31 Aug	Brands Hatch (F3)	DIS
7 Sept	Donington	R
13 Sept	Spa (F3)	8
21 Sept	Oulton Park	6
28 Sept	Zolder (F3)	10
5 Oct	Silverstone (F3)	5

Lucas British Formula 3: A. Wallace 121, M. Sala 83, M. Donnelly 59
(Herbert 15th, 8)

1987 Reynard-VW. Championship: Lucas British Formula 3

15 Mar	Thruxton	P/FL/1
5 Apr	Brands Hatch	FL/1
12 Apr	Silverstone	P/3
20 Apr	Thruxton	P/FL/1
4 May	Silverstone	P/FL/1
17 May	Brands Hatch	2
25 May	Thruxton	P/R
30 May	GP of Monaco (F3)	3
7 June	Silverstone	1
28 June	Zandvoort	9
5 July	Donington	P/R
12 July	Silverstone	4
2 Aug	Snetterton	3
9 Aug	Donington	R
15 Aug	Oulton Park	2
31 Aug	Silverstone	7
6 Sept	Brands Hatch	5
13 Sept	Spa	R
4 Oct	Silverstone (Euro F3 Cup)	R
11 Oct	Brands Hatch (Cellnet F3)	P/1
18 Oct	Thruxton	FL/3
29 Nov	Macau F3 GP	18

Lucas British F3: Herbert 79, B. Gachot 64, M. Donnelly 61

1988 Reynard-Cosworth. Championship: FIA International Formula 3000

17 Apr	Jerez	P/1
8 May	Vallelunga	R
5 June	Silverstone	7
26 June	Monza	FL/3
17 July	Enna	R
21 Aug	Brands Hatch	P/R

FIA International F3000: R. Moreno 43, O. Grouillard 34,
M. Donnelly 30 (Herbert eighth, 13)

1989 Benetton B188, except Belgium and Portugal (Tyrrell 018) and Fuji (Porsche 962). Championships: Formula 1, Fuji 1000 Challenge

26 Mar	Brazil GP, Rio	4
23 Apr	San Marino GP, Imola	11
7 May	Monaco GP, Monte Carlo	14
28 May	Mexico GP, Mexico City	15
4 June	US GP, Phoenix	5
18 June	Canada GP, Montreal	DNQ
27 Aug	Belgium GP, Spa	R
24 Sept	Portugal GP, Estoril	DNQ
8 Oct	Fuji 1000 Challenge	6

Formula 1: A. Prost 81 (76 counting), A. Senna 60, R. Patrese 40 (Herbert joint 14th, 5)

1990 Reynard, except Japan and Australia GPs (Lotus 102) and All-Japan Sports (Porsche 962). All races All-Japan F3000 except where stated

4 Mar	Suzuka	R
15 Apr	Fuji	10
13 May	Nishi-Nihon	R
27 May	Suzuka	R
22 July	Fuji (All-Japan Sports)	4
29 July	Sugo	7
26 Aug	Suzuka (All-Japan Sports)	R
2 Sept	Fuji	5
23 Sept	Suzuka	6
7 Oct	Fuji (All-Japan Sports)	R
21 Oct	Japan GP, Suzuka	R
4 Nov	Australia GP, Adelaide	R
18 Nov	Suzuka	R

Formula 1: Senna 78, Prost 71 (73), N. Piquet 43 (44) (Herbert no points)
All-Japan: K. Hoshino 58 (63), H. Ogawa 34, M. Martini 29 (Herbert joint 16th, 3)

1991 Grands Prix, Lotus 102B; All-Japan F 3000, Ralt-Mugen;
Le Mans and All-Japan Sports, 1.3r Mazda 787B. All races All-Japan
F3000 except where stated

3 Mar	Suzuka	5
24 Mar	Autopolis	7
14 Apr	Fuji	R
12 May	Mine	2
26 May	Suzuka	R
2 June	Canada GP, Montreal	DNQ
16 June	Mexico GP, Mexico City	10
22–23 June	Le Mans 24 Hours	1
7 July	France GP, Magny-Cours	10
14 July	Britain GP, Silverstone	14
21 July	Fuji (All-Japan Sports)	4
28 July	Sugo (All-Japan Sports)	R
11 Aug	Fuji	R
25 Aug	Belgium GP, Spa	7
22 Sept	Portugal GP, Estoril	R
29 Sept	Suzuka (All-Japan Sports)	7
6 Oct	Fuji (All-Japan Sports)	4
20 Oct	Japan GP, Suzuka	R
3 Nov	Australia GP, Adelaide	11
17 Nov	Suzuka (All-Japan Sports)	R
30 Nov	Fuji (All-Japan Sports)	6

Formula 1: Senna 96, N. Mansell 72, Patrese 53 (Herbert no points)
All-Japan F3000: U. Katayama 40, R. Cheever 27, V. Weidler 25
(Herbert 10th, 9)
All-Japan Sports: K. Hosino, T. Suzuki 87, H. Ogawa, M. Sekiya 85
(Herbert joint 16th, 20)

1992 Lotus 102D-Ford (Lotus 107-Ford from Imola)

1 Mar	South Africa GP, Kyalami	6
22 Mar	Mexico GP, Mexico	7
5 Apr	Brazil GP, Interlagos	R
3 May	Spain GP, Barcelona	R
17 May	San Marino GP, Imola	R

31 May	Monaco GP, Monte Carlo	R
14 June	Canada GP, Montreal	R
5 July	France GP, Magny-Cours	6
12 July	Britain GP, Silverstone	R
26 July	Germany GP, Hockenheim	R
16 Aug	Hungary GP, Hungaroring	R
30 Aug	Belgium GP, Spa	13
13 Sept	Italy GP, Monza	R
27 Sept	Portugal GP, Estoril	R
25 Oct	Japan GP, Suzuka	R
8 Nov	Australia GP, Adelaide	13

*Championship: Mansell 108, Patrese 56, Schumacher 53
(Herbert joint 14th, 2)*

1993 Lotus 107B-Ford

14 Mar	South Africa GP, Kyalami	R
28 Mar	Brazil GP, Interlagos	4
11 Apr	Europe GP, Donington	4
25 Apr	San Marino GP, Imola	8
9 May	Spain GP, Barcelona	R
23 May	Monaco GP, Monte Carlo	R
13 June	Canada GP, Montreal	10
4 July	France GP, Magny-Cours	R
11 July	Britain GP, Silverstone	4
25 July	German GP, Hockenheim	10
15 Aug	Hungary GP, Hungaroring	R
29 Aug	Belgium GP, Spa	5
12 Sept	Italy GP, Monza	R
26 Sept	Portugal GP, Estoril	R
24 Oct	Japan GP, Suzuka	11
7 Nov	Australia GP, Adelaide	R

Championship: Prost 99, Senna 73, D. Hill 69 (Herbert ninth, 11)

1994 Lotus 107C-Mugen Honda (from Barcelona, Lotus 109-Mugen Honda); Ligier JS39B-Renault at Jerez; Benetton B194-Ford in Japan and Australia

27 Mar	Brazil GP, Interlagos	7
17 Apr	Pacific GP, Aida	7
1 May	San Marino GP, Imola	10
15 May	Monaco GP, Monte Carlo	R
29 May	Spain GP, Barcelona	R
12 June	Canada GP, Montreal	8
3 July	France GP, Magny-Cours	7
10 July	Britain GP, Silverstone	12
31 July	Germany GP, Hockenheim	R
14 Aug	Hungary GP, Hungaroring	R
28 Aug	Belgium GP, Spa	12
11 Sept	Italy GP, Monza	R
25 Sept	Portugal GP, Estoril	11
16 Oct	Europe GP, Jerez	8
6 Nov	Japan GP, Suzuka	R
13 Nov	Australia GP, Adelaide	R

Championship: Schumacher 92, Hill 91, G. Berger 41 (Herbert no points)

1995 Benetton B195-Renault

26 Mar	Brazil GP, Interlagos	R
9 Apr	Argentine GP, Buenos Aires	4
30 Apr	San Marino GP, Imola	7
14 May	Spain GP, Barcelona	2
28 May	Monaco GP, Monte Carlo	4
11 June	Canada GP, Montreal	R
2 July	France GP, Magny-Cours	R
16 July	Britain GP, Silverstone	1
30 July	Germany GP, Hockenheim	4
13 Aug	Hungary GP, Hungaroring	4
27 Aug	Belgium GP, Spa	7
10 Sept	Italy GP, Monza	1
24 Sept	Portugal GP, Estoril	7

1 Oct	Europe GP, Nurburgring	5
22 Oct	Pacific GP, Aida	6
29 Oct	Japan GP, Suzuka	3
12 Nov	Australia GP, Adelaide	R

*Championship: Schumacher 102, Hill 69, D. Coulthard 49
(Herbert fourth, 45)*

1996 Sauber C15-Ford

10 Mar	Australia GP, Melbourne	DNS
31 Mar	Brazil GP, Interlagos	R
7 Feb	Argentine GP, Buenos Aires	9
28 Apr	Europe GP, Nurburgring	7
5 May	San Marino GP, Imola	R
19 May	Monaco GP, Monte Carlo	3
2 June	Spain GP, Barcelona	R
16 June	Canada GP, Montreal	7
30 June	France GP, Magny-Cours	DIS
14 July	Britain GP, Silverstone	9
28 July	Germany GP, Hockenheim	R

Other titles in this series:

EDDIE IRVINE
by Adam Cooper

DAMON HILL
From Zero to Hero
by Alan Henry

JACQUES VILLENEUVE
In His Own Right
by Christopher Hilton

JEAN ALESI
Beating the Odds
by Christopher Hilton

DAVID COULTHARD
The Flying Scotsman
by Jim Dunn

NIGEL MANSELL
The Lion at Bay
by Christopher Hilton

MICHAEL SCHUMACHER
Defending the Crown
by Christopher Hilton

AYRTON SENNA
by Christopher Hilton

JAMES HUNT
Portrait of a Champion
by Christopher Hilton